A.B.C. Antiques and Books
Territorial Road
Monticello, Minn. 55362

Antique
Tin & Tole Ware

FRONTISPIECE. *This peacock is a rare tinsmith's sign. An absolutely unique example of early nineteenth century American folk art, it was found in Torrington, Connecticut. It is made of zinc, cut out and hammered. It is about twenty-seven inches high. From the Downtown Gallery, New York.*

Antique

Tin & Tole Ware

ITS HISTORY AND ROMANCE

by Mary Earle Gould

with a foreword by

R. W. G. Vail

CHARLES E. TUTTLE COMPANY
RUTLAND, VERMONT

Representatives
Continental Europe: BOXERBOOKS, INC., *Zurich*
British Isles: PRENTICE-HALL INTERNATIONAL, INC., *London*
Australasia: PAUL FLESCH & CO., PTY. LTD., *Melbourne*
Canada: M. G. HURTIG LTD., *Edmonton*

Published by the Charles E. Tuttle Company, Inc.
of Rutland, Vermont & Tokyo, Japan
with editorial offices at
Suido 1-chome, 2-6, Bunkyo-ku, Tokyo, Japan

Copyright in Japan, 1957 by Charles E. Tuttle Co., Inc.

Library of Congress Catalog Card No. 57-8796

International Standard Book No. 0-8048-0026-X

First edition, 1958
Fourth printing, 1972

PRINTED IN JAPAN

To My Friends of

The Early American Industries Association

Contents

List of Illustrations

List of Illustrations x

Foreword

THERE have been many books on the charm and beauty of our early American household furnishings—the silver, glass, furniture, and textiles of our ancestors—but these were, for the most part, the furnishings of the stately parlors and dining rooms of the wealthy; the halls, the ballrooms, and the bedrooms of the affluent. But, nearly a quarter of a century ago, Mary Earle Gould began to collect and study the household utensils of the plain people of our country, the farmers and mechanics, the keepers of crossroad stores and village shops, the simple folk of Yankee origin who fought our wars, pushed back our frontiers, and were the backbone of our expanding economy.

Having assembled a great collection of over twelve thousand pieces of home, shop, and farm tools and utensils in wood, iron, and tin, it was inevitable that Miss Gould should eventually be recognized as an authority on the simpler but none the less interesting and important furnishings of our more modest homes, and that she should write about them. She began writing authori-

tative articles on woodenware as early as 1934 and eventually put in permanent form her vast knowledge of the subject in her volume on *Early American Wooden Ware*, which appeared, with its many fascinating illustrations, in 1942 with a revised edition six years later. She immediately became known as "the wooden lady," and her book is still the only authoritative volume on the subject.

Since our pioneer life centered around the kitchen and its great fireplace, it was only natural that Miss Gould should add to her hobby the collecting of the other furnishings of this center of the farm and village life of the eighteenth and nineteenth centuries, the ironware and tinware of our ancestors. This expanded interest resulted in the publishing, in 1949, of *The Early American House*, another well written and illustrated volume showing the ingenuity, skill, and charm of the farmers, the blacksmiths, and the tinsmiths of our early communities, who made the sturdier tools and utensils of their daily life, furnishings which are now eagerly collected by their descendants. And now our wise and enthusiastic author has completed her trilogy on the household arts with this newest book, which immediately takes its place as the one authority on its subject.

You can imagine how much this excellent history of the making of tin, its alloys, and its household products interests me personally when I tell you that my Revolutionary ancestor, Jabish Hart of Kensington, Connecticut, was a tinsmith as well as a farmer and that I am the proud owner of a conical candle lantern which he made after he became a pioneer in western New York after 1790. Being myself of the horse-and-buggy vintage, I can well remember the Yankee tin peddlers who travelled the back roads in my boyhood and who were the rivals of my own family whose country store was well stocked with a variety of shiny tinware of all sorts.

It is fascinating to learn from this scholarly and altogether delightful volume how tin was mined, worked, and fashioned into the practical and often beautiful dishes and utensils of the past. No one who has ever visited the great Winterthur Museum in Delaware will ever speak slightingly of tinware, for he will remember the wonderful display of tole which he saw and admired there. Our native workmen, who learned much from the German, Japanese, and English craftsmen in this medium, turned out many a piece of rare beauty of form and decoration, which can well stand comparison with the artistry of pieces fabricated from more precious metals.

Here you will find a bewildering array of practical forms and uses, a lavish selection of photographs of the tinware of our earlier days which tell not only of the ingenuity and skill of our forefathers but of their love of beauty as well. From the woodenware, the ironware, and the tinware of other days you can reconstruct the lives, the crafts, and the tastes of our predecessors. By visiting our historical museums where these folk arts are treasured and by building your own collection you can learn much of our past and add greatly to your own appreciation and enjoyment of the simple furnishings of farm and village, which Mary Earle Gould has done so much to save from unmerited oblivion.

R.W.G. VAIL

The New York Historical Society

Preface

Because of a chance acquisition of a wooden cheesebox, I developed an intense interest in woodenware. I went into homes on invitation and asked to be taken into the kitchens. I saw old kitchens, pantries, butteries, and sheds and I revelled in the opportunity of uncovering much that was unknown even to the owners. I learned of pieces handed down from one generation to another, and much history was given to me of those olden times and of the older folk who created and used woodenware.

Once within those early kitchens, I realized I was standing on floorboards worn by the feet of many generations and I was seeing the heart of the homes. The huge fireplaces with wide chimney throats and broad hearths were always a revelation to me, and the iron utensils standing before the fire were a source of untold history, mute evidence of the struggles and hardships of our ancestors.

The study of iron seemed to vie with that of wood, and I gradually acquired a second collection within my own museum.

I learned about the creations of the blacksmiths, and although their ware was not as numerous as was woodenware, both of these household necessities were linked together in the daily living in the early kitchens.

I always said that if I had not been led into collecting wooden articles, I would have chosen those of tin. There seemed to be so much tinware whichever way I turned, in homes and museums, some gaily painted and others shining with a brilliance. A few rare acquisitions came to my museum; one a candleholder that once hung in the cabin of a whaling vessel; another, a tin warming pan warmed by hot water; a third, a lamp used by a Civil War nurse in the field or for heating the baby's milk at home. These pieces vividly brought to me such creations of the tinsmith, and I learned that he was as important in the community as the wood turner and the blacksmith had been.

It did not take me long to see the need of research work in the field of tin. Two friends in different localities and at different times urged me to add a book on tin to my books on wood and iron. I have begun at the beginning of the making of tin plate and have shown by words and pictures the use of tin in the early homes. I again show you the life in those early kitchens and the life of our ancestors.

With the completion of this book I have endeavored to give to my friends a series of books on wood, iron, and tin. *Early American Wooden Ware*, *The Early American House*, and this volume, *Antique Tin & Tole Ware*, all written from my museum now numbering twelve hundred pieces.

With much gratitude to John B. Newlon of Amherst, Massachusetts, a retired professor with an antique shop and a forge;

to the late Frank King Swain of Doylestown, Pennsylvania; to Mrs. Gillian W. B. Bailey, of Harriman, New York; and to Mrs. Mary Johnson, of Barre, Massachusetts, a decorator of tinware.

I add a few books I used for reference: Philip William Flower, *History of the Trade in Tin*; Richardson Wright, *Hawkers and Walkers in Everyday Life*; J. L. Bishop, *History of American Manufactures*; Henry C. Mercer, *Light and Fire Making*; Arthur H. Hayward, *Colonial Lighting*; Marion Caroline Crawford, *Social Life in Old New England*; L. M. A. Roy, *The Candle Book*.

M<small>ARY</small> E<small>ARLE</small> G<small>OULD</small>

Worcester, Massachusetts

Antique
Tin & Tole Ware

CHAPTER ONE

Tin, Tin Alloys & Tin Plate

INWARE attracts attention, perhaps, only in conjunction with other household primitives. Although tinware may not seem important enough to consider, tin played a very useful part in the lives of our parents and grandparents.

Back of woodenware was the life of our ancestors in the kitchens, sheds, and barns. Back of the iron utensils and implements was the hearth, the center of the home. Tinware played as important a part in the home, following woodenware and iron utensils, and there is scarcely a home but what has some pieces of tinware used a generation and more ago.

Our interest in household tinware goes back to the basic element, the tin plate itself, from which the various tin articles were made. A brief description of how sheet iron was tinned to make tin plate is necessary in order to understand the nature of tinware and how it was created.

As an introduction, let me quote from Philip William Flower in his *History of the Trade in Tin:* "One of the earliest require-

ments of imperfect human nature was obviously a knife, a tool or a weapon of some sort for the purpose of self-protection and for the assistance of the owner in obtaining and preparing such food as he consumed." The first stage in the development of man was the Stone Age, and "civilization dates only from the discovery of fire and water; the first use of metals was the starting point of progress." The first metal to be used following the Stone Age was copper, followed by bronze, which in turn gave way to iron.

Shortly after the discovery of metals must have come the knowledge of the advantages to be obtained from their combination. Brass, an alloy of tin and copper, is frequently spoken of in the Book of Moses, and bronzes from Austria and Egypt exist today, although of unrecorded date.

For domestic use, copper, iron, brass, and even tin-coated copper were used by the luxurious Romans. "The serpent of brass which Moses caused to be lifted up in the wilderness, the pots, the shovels, the fleshhooks and the fire-pans all made of brass were employed in the temple; the jewels of silver, the jewels of gold which were borrowed from the Egyptians by the Israelites when they went out of Egypt are things which have been familiar to all of us from our earliest infancy, but possibly few if any of us have considered or cared to inquire from whence came these metals, thus early and of such importance in the history of the world."*

Brass is an alloy of tin and copper in the proportion of one part of tin and nine of copper. Genesis fixes the discovery and use of both of these elements as between 4004 and 1635 B.C. The Book of Kings, written in 1015 B.C. says: "King Solomon sent and fetched Hiram out of Tyre. He was a widow's son of the tribe Naphtali and his father was a man of Tyre, a worker in brass; and he was filled with wisdom and understanding, and cunning to work all works in brass." Hiram made pillars, temples, baths, pots, shovels, and tin basons (basins) some cast and some of wrought brass, all of which were prepared for the temple of King Solomon. This temple of King Solomon's proves that brass and tin existed in Tyre a thousand years before the Christian era.

The Phoenicians made rare dyes; tin dissolved in muriatic acid produced a brilliant purple, and tin dissolved in nitric acid made the "British scarlet." They imported tin from Cornwall, England, beginning in 450 B.C.

Cornwall furnished most of the tin that was used to make brass, which was so much sought after in the Eastern markets from the earliest ages. Britons worked the earth

* Philip William Flower, *History of the Trade in Tin.*

for tin, the ground being rocky, with earthy veins. They melted the tin ore, purified it, and cast it into the form of what they called knucklebones, which were transported strapped to the saddles of horses. Outside of England are ten small islands called Cassiterides. Tin was found early in the soil of these islands, and the name of the islands is derived from the Greek word *kassiteros,* meaning tin. Today common tin ore in the form of crystals containing seventy-eight per cent pure tin is called cassiterite.

Tin was found in subterranean veins or streams and in mines. A divining rod was used to find the stream of tin, cut from hazel rods, which were also used for making fishing rods. Apple-tree suckers, peach-tree branches, or oak of one-year growth could be used as well. Two separate shoots were fastened together instead of using one stick with one crotch, since by this method the two arms of the fork could be made exactly the same size.

Block tin is pure, refined tin cast into molds. The workmen reduced the ore to powder, the heavy metallic particles separated by immersing in water. The ore was then taken to a stamping mill and made into the state of a coarse powder. This was washed and sifted, roasted in a furnace with a moderate fire, washed and sifted again. What was obtained after this process was pure ore. Next it went into a smelting furnace with a very strong heat for seven or eight hours, the whole mass becoming fused into a molten liquid. The liquid ran off into an iron kettle with a hole near the bottom, leaving the slag or impurities behind. The tin was ladled into molds. Refined once more, it came out as pure tin. This was

PLATE 1. *Interior of an ironworks in England in 1714.* A) *is the furnace where the iron bars were heated,* B) *shows the heated bars being hammered out on an anvil. The large triphammer on the right was later used before placing them in another furnace, standing on their edges. The insertion* S) *shows the flattened bars stacked between rods. At the bottom can be seen the big shears used to cut the plates with and the finished plates. (From Philip William Flower,* History of the Trade in Tin.)

poured into granite molds to be cast as block tin.

Grain tin is another kind. Stream tin was dressed by poundings and washings and taken to a blast furnace, where it was subjected to a powerful heat. Melted, it was taken to an iron kettle under which was a gentle fire and it was kept in agitation by plunging in pieces of charcoal soaked in water. The charcoal remained at the bottom of the kettle, the water in it turned to vapor, the impurities were thrown to the surface and skimmed off, and the pure metal was

removed by ladles into molds, to form blocks, which were known as grain tin.

Iron was brought to the mills in little bars. The iron that had been made with charcoal, known as charcoal iron, was considered better than that which had been made with coke, called coke iron. The bars were first heated in a furnace and then hammered out on an anvil and then placed under a large hammer, until they were twice as broad and long as before. Then, as plates, they were dipped in water which contained a sandy earth mixed with charcoal dust to prevent adhesion. They were then taken to another furnace, where they were placed vertically side by side on their edges, resting on two bars of iron which supported them. They were surrounded by large pieces of charcoal, which were ignited. When the bundle was sufficiently heated, a lot of forty was taken out and placed under a hammer that weighed seven hundred pounds. The position of the sheets was changed, for the outside sheets cooled more rapidly than the inner ones. After the hammering, they were heated again. This time they were taken in lots of one hundred, divided into two parts. Once more they were hammered, once more placed in the heat, and again hammered for the third and last time.

The sheets were then squared with shears and measured for length. They were then placed on red-hot bars lying on the ground, with two thick bars placed on top. The big hammer was then used again to give the sheets their last polish. The squared sheets went to the cellar, and the imperfect ones were sold as sheet iron.

The plates in the cellar were scrubbed with sandstone and then put into vats of water soured with barley or rye. This operation was called "pickling." The water had fermented because of the heat generated by the furnace, and this removed the scales left from the forge. The sheets remained in the vats for seventy-two hours and were turned and re-turned. Then they were taken out and rubbed by women with sand and water, using a cork and rag. Now ready for tinning, they were kept immersed in water.

The "tin pot" was nineteen and one-half inches in diameter, made of cast iron. It was filled with tin, water, and tallow. The fire under the pot burned sixteen to seventeen hours. The tin was taken with a ladle and poured from a great height back into the pot, this being done several times. To test the heat of the tin pot, a pickled sheet of iron was dipped into the liquid metal. If the tin coating on it turned out yellow, the metal was too hot; it had to be silvery white.

The pot was divided into two sections by a heavy sheet. Tallow and pure water were then added, causing the contents of the pot to swell and foam. One hundred sheets, still wet from the water bath, were placed with tongs flat under the tin. Then one hundred more were put in. These were left for fifteen minutes, moved about with a wooden stick. The tallow on top was skimmed off and saved in a vessel. A man removed one sheet at a time with tongs and placed it vertically upon two bars of iron from which extended two rows of spikes which held the sheets. Another workman took one sheet at a time and dipped it into the smaller section of the pot. Each sheet was carefully removed and placed on a grate of iron and left to drain, fourteen of them each time. A little boy took out one sheet and gave it to a woman who cleared off the grease with a piece of stuff and then with sawdust. Another little boy put in a sheet as soon as one was taken out, keeping the pot filled with the same number of sheets. When one hundred sheets had been taken from the bath, the tin that had dripped off and the tallow that had been skimmed off were put back into the pot, fresh water was added, and the operation was then repeated.

After the sheets had been cleaned with sawdust, they were carried to a room with

PLATE 2. *Interior of a tin-plate factory in England in 1714. In the right-hand corner are shown the "pickling" vats, where the iron plates were placed before the tinning prcoess. To the left a man is placing the plates in the "tin pot". In the center a woman is scrubbing the iron plates taken from the tin pot with rags and sawdust. At the top a group of women are cleaning the finished tin plates with oatmeal. (From Philip William Flower,* History of the Trade in Tin.*)*

a stove in it, to be kept warm. A woman rubbed them with oatmeal, using an old piece of linen, and another woman completed the operation with more rubbing. The lower edges of the sheets were thicker and full of drops. A pot of pure tin with a fire under it was standing ready, and the plates were dipped in to remove the drops. A little boy dipped one after another, and they were taken out by a man who rubbed them with moss. Then thirty or forty sheets were placed together and beaten above and below with a mallet on a block of wood, to pack them closer. They were bent a little in the

middle to better fit into the packing boxes. The defective sheets were taken out and sold later at a lower price.

The tin plates were made in two sizes, eleven and seven-eighths by nine inches and eighteen and three-eighths by eleven and three-eighths inches. One and one-tenth pounds of tallow and sixteen pounds of tin were used for three hundred small sheets and twice that amount for the larger sheets. Tinning was done twice a week; eighteen hundred sheets were tinned, rubbed, and packed into boxes in five hours. The boxes were made of elm, which is tough and flexible enough to take nails without splitting.

The particular town or village in northern Germany where the manufacture of tin plates originated and the actual year in which tinning began are unknown. But it has been clearly ascertained that in 1620, the trade had already existed for many years in Bohemia. The knowledge of this manufacture was obtained by the Duke of Saxony, who began the manufacturing in his own territories, and it was from Saxony that the secret came to England in 1670. Pontypool took up the manufacture. But because of many civil troubles, it was not until 1720 that the making of tin plate was well established. In 1728, John Payne invented a process for rolling flat or sheet rolls for the manufacture of iron for tin plates. In 1783, Henry Cort discovered the idea of grooved rolls, but it was not appreciated for a number of years.

Better methods were produced as the years went on. In 1720, the iron plates were scoured with sand and water and the rough spots filed off. The plates were then coated with resin before dipping in tin. In 1747, a new process was introduced: after the plates had been cold rolled, they were soaked for a week in lees of bran, which had become acid by fermentation, remaining in the liquid for ten days. The plates were then scoured with sand and water, with much better results. These later methods were changed slightly to facilitate the work.

There seemed to be a difference in the grade of tin coming from Cornwall and from Singapore. The Cornwall tin came in the shape of refined blocks, which weighed as much as four hundred pounds. The foreign tin from Singapore or Java was bought in ingots, both the color and the runs being thinner. In dipping, it was the English tin that was used in the first dipping and the foreign tin for the second, being of better color and more fluid. The quantity of tin used at a tin-plate works was five tons weekly for two thousand boxes of plates.

The sorting of the tin plates was done on iron-faced tables. Some had to go back to the tinhouse while others were called wasters and sent off to be used for different purposes. This work was done by girls. The plates were counted, weighed, and fastened in boxes which were branded with a hot iron. Again, charcoal tin was superior to that made with coke.

In 1670, Pontypool began the manufacture of a certain ware. The method was discovered by Thomas Allgood. He extracted copperas and oil from coal and invented the method of lacquering iron plates with a brilliant varnish. Allgood died before he had perfected the method, but the work was carried on by his son Edward. Finally, there was established a manufactory of japan-ware which was unrivalled for many years. Similar establishments were begun at Usk by a branch of the family, and it was from these two places that the beautiful tin trays were exported and which today are examples of the finest art in tin in this country.

The most useful alloy in the arts has been brass. It has been considered next to iron in importance. It was usually made of equal parts of copper and zinc, although some times there were as many as five parts of copper to one of zinc. The ancients in the Bible were acquainted with it, and the Romans made use of it. Musical instruments, vessels, implements, ornaments, and even gates were made from brass. It has been questioned if it could have been brass as it is generally known, for zinc was not discovered as a separate metal until the sixteenth century. Commonly known to us today are brass warming pans, bells, vessels, and pails and many ornaments of brass that came from the old country in the early years.

Bronze is an alloy of copper and tin with equal parts of each or as much as ten parts of copper and one of tin. Roman vessels were made of copper and were coated inside with tin to prevent the oxidation of copper, which is quite poisonous. The brass referred to in the Bible was undoubtedly bronze. The ancient nations used bronze not only for objects of art but for a great number of practical implements.

Pewter was used for quality utensils more than is the practice today. It is a tin alloy, commonly consisting of four parts of tin and one of lead. Poor quality pewter with greater lead content is discernible by the difference in color and softness. American pewter differed from the English variety in the amount of lead used. During the Civil War days, pewter utensils were taken and melted to extract the lead for bullets. The number of pewter articles made across the Atlantic and in this country add up to a long list, and the pieces are greatly valued by their owners. The pewter of England bears an English stamp, and that of this country has a mark, although some of the earlier products had no mark.

An alloy that followed pewter was britan-nia. This consists of ninety parts of tin, eight of antimony, and two of copper. This was used in household articles in the same manner as pewter, but more commonly. It was at first stamped with dies and soldered into shape. Later, however, the spinning method was introduced. In this process, a thin sheet of britannia was placed on a wooden model shaped like the article to be made. The model was rotated on a lathe, while the metal was pressed into shape against the model with tools. Britannia was also used as a base for German silver, which was produced for the first time in 1840.

In America, Edward Patterson established the first manufactory of tinware in Berlin, Connecticut in 1770. His tin plate was imported from England. Patterson went back to Ireland and brought his brother William, and the two worked together at the trade. They peddled their wares in baskets and on horse-back, covering many miles, going from door to door. For the duration of the Revolutionary War the business was suspended, but immediately following these years ten thousand boxes of tinned plate were manufactured into culinary vessels, and twelve tin shops were listed in Berlin. This was in 1815. There are two spellings of their family name. According to the records, the Pattersons remained in Connecticut and the Pattisons migrated to New Jersey.

In 1774, a convention assembled at Philadelphia to propose the establishment of tin-plate manufacture, considering both the manufacture and the trade. At that time there was not sufficient tin even to make the canteens and kettles for the army. In 1775, a Thomas Mayberry carried on the manufacture of sheet iron at Mount Holley, Pennsylvania. In that year, Congress ordered from him five tons of sheet iron for the use of Thomas Bales, a blacksmith, who proposed to supply the Continental troops with camp kettles of that material, provided he could have credit for that quantity of sheet iron.

A sheet iron manufactory was established in 1776 by Murray, Griffin and Bullard who made camp kettles, blaze pans, tea-kettles and other wares. Such wares had been made many years earlier by Cornelius Bradford from block or pure tin and from pewter. Plymouth and Bristol in Massachusetts had seven rolling and slitting mills in 1798, for making sheet iron for tinware, producing tin in large quantities. In 1810, United States had three hundred and sixteen triphammers and thirty-four rolling and slitting mills which required sixty-five hundred tons of iron.

Iron was found in small quantities in this country in various places, but because sheet iron was imported from England at such a low price, both because of the better developed mines and the cheaper labor, sheet iron was made in this country only in inconsequential amounts.

Tinware continued to be made until toward the end of the nineteenth century and the greatest amount was produced after the Civil War. It was then that fireplaces and iron utensils gave way to cookstoves and tinware, and the mode of living changed. Tinware often in use today and tinware that is collected and preserved are both subject to the tin disease, because of the rust of the iron below the surface. Because of this disease, early tinware and toleware in good condition is scarce and hard to find. It helped bring to a close the long period when tin graced the pantry and the home, the church and the school.

CHAPTER TWO

Tin on the Hearth

BEFORE the blazing logs on the hearth stood an odd array of iron utensils. There were few cooking utensils in the possession of the new colonists when they began living in their new homes, but they seemed to be sufficient for the housewife.

Iron utensils were brought from old England along with a few of copper and brass, the various names of which are found in inventories and wills. The allotment was very small, as each ship sailed from England. But when iron foundries began to produce implements and tools in the new country by 1643, the hearth boasted of hand-wrought ironware. Pots—from the small ones that held one quart to the large cauldrons holding gallons—skillets, teakettles, spiders, oat-cake plates, toasters, the waffle iron and the wafer iron, fish broilers, gridirons, rabbit roasters, Dutch ovens, long-handled frying pans and long-legged trivets, toddy irons and various spatulas and forks with long handles—these made up the iron family. They never wore out; they were passed from one generation to another and they presented a drab appearance on the hearth, in front of the cavernous fireplace.*

If one searched through diaries—it was a common thing to keep diaries—one might run across an entry in the late eighteenth century that read something like this: "When my father brought home a tin reflector oven, we all rejoiced to see the shiny utensil standing on the hearth, giving us a bit of joy in the drab kitchen." Those first ovens were called reflector ovens, for the heat from the fire on the hearth before which the oven was placed reflected from its curved back, thus providing heat both from the front and from the back.

Probably the first reflector oven was the tin roasting oven (1790), called the tin kitchen. The word kitchen comes from the Old English word, "kichen," meaning to cook; the tin kitchen was a cooker. It was made in various sizes for small families and for large families, for small roasts and for large roasts. One was scarcely a foot long,

* Gould, *The Early American House.*

PLATES 3 & 4. *Front and rear views of a tin kitchen, or roasting oven, showing spit and skewers.*

while others were as much as three feet long. The typical example shown here is made half-cylindrical in shape, standing on four feet; the back legs are doubled strips of tin and the front feet are of wire, a continuation of the wire that runs down the sides of the oven, beginning with a loop at the top. One side of the oven has a slanting slot and the other a center hole surrounded by a circle of holes. The spit, running through the oven, holds the meat. It is a rod of iron with a sharp point at one end and a U-shaped projection at right angles at the other end, which fits into the circle of holes. The rod has three or four slots for the skewers. There is a door at the back that lifts, through which the roast could be watched or basted. Sometimes the family's initials were perforated on the door.

The process of roasting a piece of meat or a large bird such as a turkey was to thrust the spit through the center hole of one side, impale the meat or bird onto it, and rest the pointed end in the slot on the opposite side. The meat or bird was then fastened to the spit with skewers, thrust through the meat and into the slots in the spit. As the meat roasted, the projection of the arm of the spit was rotated until all sides were roasted. To remove the roast, the wire that passed over the slot was pulled out, opening the slot. These wires are often rusted and cannot be moved except by thorough oiling. The skewers were pulled out of the meat and the roast slid off the spit onto a platter. Skewers were kept on holders, like the one shown here, which has two arms to hold a set of six. A projection extends by which the holder was hung by the fire, ready for use. Today, holders such as these are quite scarce and often sell for as much as forty-five dollars for a set.

The juice of the meat dripped into the curved bottom of the roaster and was poured out through a snout. Gravy was made for the roast or served later in stew. This tin kitchen is often used today in old taverns, when guests ask that the meat or fowl be roasted in the old manner. And following the old manner, too, turkeys are roasted in the side brick oven, taking long hours as would be necessary. A fire is built in the oven itself, heating the bricks white hot, the charred embers taken out, the oven swept, and the large pan holding the turkeys set within. This takes about nine hours. There is romance in using the old utensils and in cooking in the old manner, bringing back the romance of the old days that cannot be had in the days of modern inventions.

Before the invention of the tin kitchen, the meat or fowl was impaled on a spit of wood or iron and hung by a cord over the fire. The cord was twisted and as it untwisted, the roast revolved and cooked on all sides. "Done to a turn" is the expression coming down the years, from the turning of the spits. Children were often given the duty of keeping the cord twisted, a very tedious job.

A mechanical device was invented whereby the spit could be automatically turned. It was called a clock jack, made with cogwheels with a spring attachment that could be wound. This jack was fastened to the

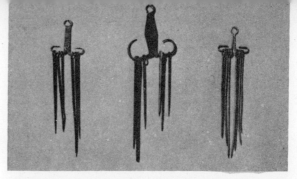

PLATE 6. *Skewers were hung on special holders of the type shown here.*

wall or mantel above the fire, and the cord holding the spit and meat revolved as the clock unwound. By pulling a chain, the clock was wound up again. Some of them were timed. Brass clock jacks were ornamental to the fireplace, polished as were all the brass and copper utensils on the hearth. Some of the clock jacks were made of iron and were elaborate arrangements, standing in front of the fire.

A drip pan or a shallow iron spider was placed under the roast to catch the juices. The juices were a very important part of the roast, for they were used a great deal in ragouts and stews. The tin drip pan looks like a dust pan except that there is a deep rim on all four sides. It was made of one sheet of tin, folded at the four corners and the edge rolled over a wire. This rolled edge was necessary on all tin utensils, to protect the edge from breaking. A tin handle was riveted to the back, and the edge of that too was

PLATE 5. *While meat was being cooked on the spit, tin drip pans like this one were placed under the meat to catch the juices.*

PLATE 7. *A rather unusual spit basket attached to a set of andirons.*

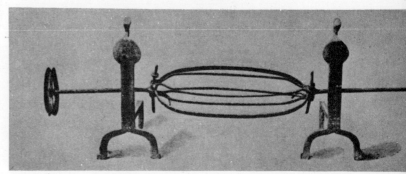

❧ 13 ❦ *Tin on the Hearth*

PLATE 8. *An assortment of early cooking utensils have been assembled to reconstruct this typical fireplace now in the Essex Museum of Salem, Massachusetts. Note the clock jack at the left.*

PLATES 9 & 10. *Two types of biscuit ovens constructed on the same principle as the roasting ovens. The pan for the biscuits is missing in the top oven.*

rolled over a wire which continued to the end to make a loop by which the pan could be hung by the chimney.

The next important tin utensil was the biscuit oven. The common type was made in the shape of a square open C, held up by strips of tin making two back legs. The lower part of the oven slopes down to the floor and the upper part acts as a cover. There are two ledges inside on which the pan for the biscuits rests. Some biscuit ovens of this type were made in one piece, while others had a cover that could be removed. The cover has two hinged strips of tin that set into two slots in the body part of the oven. Handles extend at the sides, so the oven could be lifted from one place to another.

The biscuits in those early days of the tin ovens were made of corn meal, called Indian meal, and water. The meal took its name from the fact that the Indians cultivated the wild-growing maize or corn and showed the first settlers how to plant and harvest their corn. Primitive methods of grinding

Antique Tin & Tole Ware ⊰ 14 ⊱

the corn were used for many years. The Indians had a hollow stone for the receptacle and another stone for a pounder, often fastening the pounder to a bough of a tree, directly over the hollow stone. The bough took the weight of the stone pounder as it was worked up and down.

In the days of near-starvation, a few kernels of corn was the allotment to each person. And when a traveller started out on a journey, he carried in his knapsack some kernels of corn. The cakes made of ground corn and water were called jonny cakes, shortened from the word journey, because they were taken on journeys. This eventually changed to Johnny cakes.

The cakes were laid on the shelf of the biscuit oven, which was placed before the fire. In the South, these coarse cakes of corn meal and water were placed on the slanting head of a hoe in front of the fire. This brought about the name of hoe cakes. And before the days of the tin biscuit ovens, the cakes in the North were baked on a wooden board propped against a kettle or on a similar board with a supporting leg projecting from the back. These cakes were called bannock cakes, and the board was called a bannock board. The cakes were coarse and dry, as they were made with a dry dough unlike the running dough used in today's makes.

When charcoal appeared in the homes, another type of tin biscuit oven was made, larger than the first oven and not of the reflector type. This was made in the style of a box on three legs or brackets and with a cover or door. At the back is a built-in holder for a pot which held a charcoal fire. This allowed the oven to be used in any

PLATES 11 & 12. *These biscuit ovens were developed after the earlier reflector types and have built-in compartments for charcoal holders that provided the heat. These were used for baking crackers.*

convenient place, not being dependent on the fire of the hearth. One such oven was found in an old home near Worcester and came to light at an auction. The cover or door to this one drops down when opened, and within are two wire shelves. A similar oven was found in an attic of an old farmhouse five miles from where the previous

Tin on the Hearth

one had been found. This second oven has a cover that lifts and has two ledges on which rests a tin pan, which fortunately was found in the oven. The pot of charcoal could be taken out to empty and to refill.

A third type of tin biscuit oven is a long, low oven with two compartments. This stands on frail six-inch legs of tin and not only has a holder for charcoal but has a hole in the back of the holder for a stovepipe which connected with the chimney, to avoid contaminating the air of the room with any disagreeable gases from the charcoal. This oven has two doors of the same type as the doors on a foot stove, fastened with a frail wire latch. And within each door are two wire racks, allowing for more biscuits to be baked at one time.

PLATE 14. *This large tin oven was used before an open fire for baking or for roasting.*

PLATE 13. *This baking oven has a compartment for a charcoal holder in the middle, which is flanked by two baking compartments, each with a door and a couple of shelves. Note the hole in the back where a chimney could be attached. Also for crackers.*

Further research has uncovered the fact that the ovens burning charcoal were for baking crackers. Charcoal gave out twice as much heat as any other fuel, which was necessary when baking the cracker dough.

The word cracker was used to designate a flat, hard biscuit, or a flat bread made dry and hard so it would preserve for a long time. Crackers were first called sea biscuits or sea bread, which is why those tin ovens were called biscuit ovens. These crackers were also known as ship biscuits, pilot biscuits, pilot bread, or Captain's biscuits. These early biscuits or crackers were made for sailors going out to sea. They were much like the hard-tack that was made of flour, water, and salt for the soldiers in the army.

These biscuit ovens were also used when food was reheated. Pies, porridge, and puddings were baked in large numbers at one time, to be laid away in the larder to freeze. Pies were stacked one upon another, often as many as fifty of them. When a pie was to be used for a meal, it was taken from the larder and put into the biscuit oven before the fire and warmed.

We find references of a "pye-woman" as well as a baker, both of whom baked in the town bakeshop situated in the cellar of a tavern. Many old taverns had large brick ovens still seen today, built in the cellar and used as an extra oven when large quantities of food had to be baked or roasted.

Bean porridge was baked in large quantities, and that too was brought out to be warmed in the ovens. But bean porridge was not always warmed over. When the families went on their mid-winter trip to the market, a chunk of bean porridge was tied to the side of the sleigh seat. Any time one of the family felt the need of something to eat, he whacked off a piece and ate until he was satisfied. Indian puddings, too, were baked in quantities and warmed over when needed. The biscuit ovens were an important addition to the hearth and were used very often. There must have been many varieties of them in the different localities.

Other tin roasters were created by the tinsmith to lighten the tasks of the housewife. There was a bird roaster on which bobwhites were roasted, hung by their breasts on hooks. The bird roaster is more commonly seen than some of the early hearth ovens. It has a flat, upright face with narrow side projections and a base with turned-up edges to catch the drippings. Seven wire hooks are attached on the inside and from the back of it projects a handle on which the roaster rested as it stood in front of the fire.

PLATE 15. *This squat tin kettle is a foot in diameter and only three inches high. It was probably used on the stove top.*

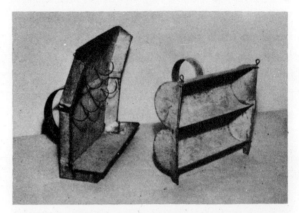

PLATE 16. *Two distinctive types of roasters used before the hearth. The one on the left was used to roast small birds such as bobwhites and quail. The one on the right is a rather rare apple roaster.*

Bobwhites or quails were very common and when roasted were considered a delicacy. Turkeys and other large birds would be roasted in the tin kitchen, but the smaller birds were hung on the hooks of the bird roaster. In the marshes and woods birds were found, such as the pheasant, partridge, woodcock, pigeon, and quail, as well as the plover, snipe, and curlew, which are not commonly found today.

A rare little tin roaster is the one with two curved shelves, resting on a handle. This was used in front of the fire when roasting apples; four apples would easily fit on each shelf. This roaster was found in

Tin on the Hearth

the old home of a school friend, where everything had not only been saved but labelled, back to four generations. If the tin apple roaster had not been labelled, it might have come into my museum as an unknown piece. As yet, I have not seen a similar one. As the two rows of apples baked before the fire, sizzling from the heat, the juices were caught in the curved shelves. It would be worth trying before an open fire today!

To warm plates before mealtime, there were tin plate-warmers. These are considered museum pieces and seldom seen. The one in my museum stands twenty-one inches high and thirteen inches wide, with a dome-shaped top and four splayed iron legs with claw feet. Large iron rings are fastened to the sides in two brass rosettes. The warmer has three shelves, is open toward the fire, and closes with a door toward the room. Bars extend down the front toward the fire so the dishes would not be pushed through and out onto the hearth. Such tin warmers were decorated, either with gold lines or with a pattern. This plate warmer came

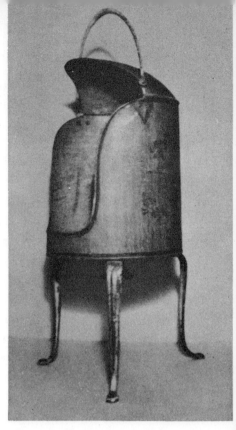

PLATE 18. *This small plate warmer is painted pumpkin yellow with designs in black.*

PLATE 17. *An interesting plate warmer with cast-iron legs and large brass rings for handles. Thirty-two inches high.*

originally from Virginia. It was brought back by a New England family when they returned to their native home after a period in Virginia. When breaking up that home, the daughter sold the warmer to me after a chance meeting at a gasoline station. We were strangers and our conversation turned toward antiques, with the resulting sale of the warmer to me. It pays to be friendly—perhaps collectors are!

Another tin plate-warmer is smaller and built differently. It has slender, splayed legs and the front has a curved opening, with no door and no shelves inside. The oven stands fifteen inches high, is painted yellow, and has a hoop handle, by which it could have been carried to a place in front of the fire or moved to one side when not in use. The plates to be warmed rested on the floor of the oven.

A small curved cover, called a tin bonnet,

open on one side and having a handle on the top, seems to have been used as a warmer for one plate of food. It could have been used to cover a pan of apples, roasting on the hearth. The stones or bricks in the hearth were undoubtedly warm all the time, and the cover must have helped in keeping things warm.

Gridirons were first made of wood, then of wire, then of iron. A tin gridiron is rare. Those of iron were quite common, made with a revolving head, square or round, riveted to a stand with three short legs and a handle. Still another type was oblong or square with grooved slats, fashioned in one piece with the legs and handle. The workmanship of these grooves suggests that these gridirons were not as old as those with revolving heads.

When tin could be used in domestic articles, a gridiron of tin was fashioned. This has slats, grooved sides, four short legs, and a handle at one side, not at the back. The two front legs are shorter, so the gridiron tips toward the front, and at the front edge is a deep cup into which the juices ran. It is a very ingenious piece for the hearth and so light in weight it would take no effort on the housewife's part to use it. Tin

PLATE 20. *This plate warmer was called a tin bonnet and would accommodate only one plateful of food, perhaps, to be kept warm for a latecomer.*

surely must have brought a relief after the years of struggling with heavy iron pots and other such implements of iron.

The fire was raked up each night in order to keep the embers alive until the following morning. A copper or brass cover was known to have existed in England which was put over the raked fire. This had perforations so that the gases from the live coals might escape and a small amount of air enter. It was called a curfew cover. The signal for raking up the fire and putting on the cover was the ringing of a bell, at eight o'clock. It was called the curfew, from the French word *couvre feu*, meaning to cover the fire. In this country, for almost a century, a bell was rung at nine o'clock as a signal to retire.

Because every fire tender could not keep

PLATE 19. *A gridiron of tin, being lightweight, was much easier to handle than those made of iron. An ingenious device, it slants forward and has a cup attached to catch the juices.*

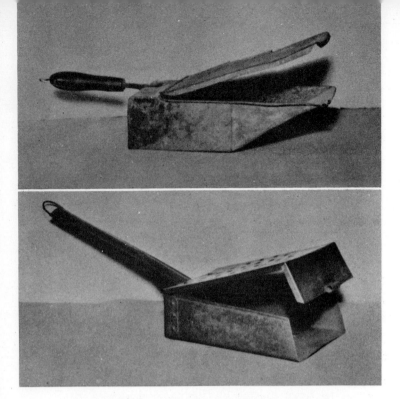

PLATES 21 & 22. *Two fire pans used to carry embers from hearth to hearth to light new fires or to rekindle lost fires. The one on top could easily be two hundred years old.*

a fire day in and day out, a fire pan or coal carrier was fashioned of sheet iron, made either by a blacksmith or a tinsmith. These pans have a short arm of iron, which is artistically riveted to the box, the arm having a pointed end that was driven into an appropriate handle of wood. The box measures about ten inches long, five inches wide, and four inches deep. The arm is seven inches long. The bottom of the pan slants up to the front edge where it meets the cover, making the box in the shape of a scoop. The hinged cover has perforations, pierced in a design, so that gasses from the live embers might escape when the box was filled.

Such a fire pan could easily be two hundred years old. There is nothing to go by in listing such a piece, but because of the workmanship, one can readily see it is one

of the earliest pieces. How we wish it might tell of its owners, of the chimney on which it hung, and of the activities in the kitchen! Perhaps it was a one-room house where it helped out when the fire was lost, or perhaps it was a two-room house with a lean-to where the daily work was carried on. It might have hung in the wing of the house where the young married daughter or son were living, carrying on under the roof of the family home. The fire pan would be taken down from the hook on the chimney jamb and it would be taken by someone of the family to a neighbor, even though many miles away. It might have been on foot or on horseback or in a sleigh. The fire pan would be brought back with live embers from the neighbor's fire, and the lost fire was then coaxed and tended in a new lot of kindling wood until a roaring fire was once more on the hearth. The fire pan was also used when kindling a fire in another room in the house or, as was the practice in the South, when embers were taken from the kitchen in the servants' quarters to kindle a fire in the master's room.

It was far easier to go a-borrowing with a fire pan than it was to strike a spark with flint, striker, and tinder. Every home had a tinderbox with the wherewithal for making a spark, but it was not every person who could make a spark. The tinderbox is a small round tin box with a cover and handle and a holder on top for the candle. In the box is a piece of flint, a shaped piece of steel called a striker, and a small cover with a ring. Any scrap of calico or linen would do for tinder, put in the bottom of the box. The steel was struck against the flint to produce a spark, which caught fire to the tinder.

Antique Tin & Tole Ware ❧ 20 ❧

The candle in the holder on the box cover was lighted from the flame, the inside small cover was used to smother the burning calico, the flint and steel put back into the box, and the cover with the lighted candle put on. In the museum is a pair of tinderboxes, one of them complete, even to the charred tinder. These tinderboxes were used long before the days of friction matches. It was not until 1834 that matches were made from splinters of pine or aspen wood and tipped with a composition containing phosphorus.

A later fire pan was made in a different style. The handle has a rolled edge, rolled over a wire hoop that was long enough to include an open end by which the pan was hung. This type is like a box with only three sides, the front end being open, leaving it shaped like a scoop. The cover has an extension in the front that takes the place of the fourth side of the box and clamps down with a catch when closed. Because another similar pan has been found with the stamp of a manufactory on it, this type appears to have been made in the period of manufacturing and not in the time of the village blacksmith and the tinsmith whose hand-wrought pieces earlier supplied the home.

Fire pans were given to a bride to take to her new home or to a new hearth in the wing of the old home. A bread peel, a wafer iron, a fire pan, and other small gifts were given to her, and she took with her a large dowry of linen, woven on the family loom. The dowry was not meant as a display of wealth but rather was a matter of necessity. Washing was done in those early years only seasonally, and the linen was required to

last the length of time between one washing and another. This part of the home life of the early settlers is discussed fully in my book *The Early American House*.

Can you imagine the delight of finding out that corn could be popped! The kernels were black in the early days. Governor Winthrop of Boston wrote in his journal in 1630 that when corn was "parched," as he called it, it turned inside out and was "white and floury within."

A small corn popper in the museum is only six inches long, five inches wide, and four inches deep. The cover is pierced with a pattern of holes and the bottom is fashioned from a fine mesh wire, crudely fastened to the turned-up bottom edges of the box. A broad, sturdy iron arm extends at the back to a distance of eight inches, the pointed tip of which was thrust into a wooden handle about sixteen inches long. Signs of its having been held over the live coals can be seen in the charred wood where the wooden handle meets the iron arm. This

PLATE 23. *In the eighteenth century, gadgets like this were devised for popping corn over the hearth. The bottom is made of wire mesh. It holds one quart.*

PLATE 24. *The early families roasted their coffee beans in roasters of this sort. This one of sheet iron, eight inches in diameter, is from the eighteenth century. It has lost its wooden handle.*

corn popper might have held a quart of popped corn, which would seem an abundance in those early days of scant supplies. And surely one can believe that this little popper was made two hundred years ago in the eighteenth century. We can picture in our minds the jolly family with the neighbors gathered around the fire on a cold winter's evening, with the winds howling down the chimney throat, with apples roasting on the hearth, waiting for the shelled corn to pop. There was a special kind of corn grown for popping corn and it was shelled in a big barrel that had a floor board perforated with holes. A heavy pounder took off the kernels.

Another popper is in Old Sturbridge Village, Sturbridge, Massachusetts. This consists of a wire-mesh cylinder, about a foot long, with solid tin ends. A long handle extends from the middle, partly iron and

partly wood. This popper held about two quarts.

Coffee-bean roasters date back to the early eighteenth century. Coffee came into the home when whaling vessels brought back coffee beans from their trips to foreign lands. The beans were boiled whole in the beginning, which made a very unsatisfactory drink. By the middle of the eighteenth century the beans were roasted, and coffee as a drink was already commonly known.

Coffee-bean roasters were wrought by the tinsmith. One in the museum is round, the box part made of a strip of sheet iron, two and one-half inches wide and about twenty-eight inches long. This strip was curved into cylindrical form, and a bottom was put on by turning the edge of the round bottom-piece onto the edge of the strip, which made the side of the box. A round cover has an extending arm of iron about ten inches long, ending in a curved tip for convenience in lifting. The box has an eighteen-inch arm of iron riveted to the side, which tapers to a point which was driven into a wooden handle, now missing. On the extension of the handle is a small piece of sheet iron, which stands out about two inches. This caught into the slot of the handle of the cover, to hold the cover securely when the coffee beans were being roasted over the fire.

The beans were ground in a coffee grinder after they had been roasted. There were many styles of grinders covering a period of many years. The grinders had a holder for the beans, a crank that ground them, and a drawer below that caught the ground coffee. Some of these grinders were handmade of tin, brass, iron, and wood. At a later time an iron grinder was made that screwed to the wall, with a patent stamp on it.

A very early coffee-bean roaster, made by a tinsmith, is in the Farmer's Museum at Cooperstown, New York. This is illustrated. Another such roaster is in Old Sturbridge Village, while another may be found in Williamsburg, Virginia. The head was made in a cylindrical shape, about a foot long and seven inches in diameter. At one side is a wide slot. Into grooves of the slot fits a sliding cover that moves up and down. An iron point three inches long extends at the bottom end, and at the other end is a long arm of iron set into a wooden handle.

In the motion picture entitled *A Day at Williamsburg*, a colored servant is shown using the roaster in the fireplace. The point rests on the hearth, and the servant is spinning the roaster around by turning the handle in his hands, shaking the beans about in the cylindrical head. Then the servant slides open the door and pours the

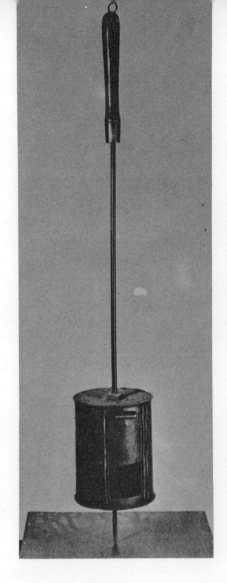

PLATE 26. *This rare coffee-bean roaster is found in the Farmer's Museum of Cooperstown, New York. The projecting point was placed on the hearth, and the cylindrical head was rotated by the long handle.*

PLATE 25. *The coffee beans were ground in primitive grinders like this one. The top on this grinder is made of brass.*

beans out of the roaster into a coffee grinder. The crank is slowly turned, and into the wooden drawer at the bottom come the grounds. The grounds are then poured into a pot of boiling water hanging on the crane, and after a certain time of boiling the coffee is ready and is poured into a coffeepot, for breakfast. The entire film records very accurately the use of the utensils and implements found on the hearth, even to the making of waffles in the old iron.

The film also shows the servant scooping up live coals from the fire with a fire pan or fire carrier. Taking the live coals into the bedroom of his master, the servant empties the pan, covers the coals with shavings, and blows on them until a blaze bursts forth. Then the fire spreads to the wood that had been prepared the night before, and all is ready for the master when he arises.

One day, at a tea in the birthplace of Clara Barton, founder of the American Red Cross, I met an acquaintance who is active in the societies connected with Clara Barton. She told me of a fire pan that had been in her mother's family. That same week, I called on my acquaintance with the hopes of purchasing the pan. It is now in my museum. The family claimed that their grandmother had carried live coals in it, and no doubt it had been used for that purpose. But its real use was for a coffee-bean roaster. That was one more proof that many things made in the early days were put to more than one use.

So, home with my so-called fire pan, I examined it and concluded it was a coffee-bean roaster. The long wooden handle was charred at the end near the head, and the stains in the pan gave me proof that it was

PLATE 27. *This is another coffee-bean roaster of unusual workmanship. This may have also been used as a fire pan to carry embers from the hearth.*

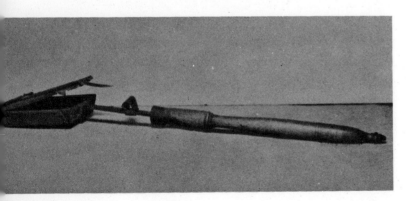

no carrier but that it had held beans roasting over the embers. The workmanship is very unusual. The box was made of one piece of thin sheet iron, folded at the corners, and was eight inches long, six inches wide, and less than two inches deep. A thin piece was riveted at the end to make a hinge to hold the cover. Riveted to the opposite end is a thin strip, an inch wide, extending about four inches like a lip. On the handle of the box is a slide which slips along to catch the extension of the cover and hold it securely when the box was closed. The handle was riveted to the bottom of the roaster, and was about seven inches long, ending in a point which was driven into a twenty-four-inch wooden handle, a brass band binding the two together.

It would not be safe to say that the round coffee-bean roaster is older than this oblong box-shaped roaster. Even though it looks more primitive, it might have been made by a less proficient workman and with less durable material. The date of any early utensil or implement cannot always be told, but it can be classified in a certain period or group of years. Both of these pieces were made in the early eighteenth century.

Another holder in the museum appears to be either a coal carrier, a coffee-bean roaster, or a corn popper. It was classified as a coal carrier, but the short handle and the stains inside the box put it in the group of roasters. Made like the tin fire carrier, which has a sheet-iron handle and perforations in the cover, it is not, however, made to scoop up live embers. Coffee-bean roasters did not have perforations in the cover, but perhaps they could have had them and been just as practical. The final conclusion was that it was used on a stove top, for either a roaster or a corn popper. Roasters of this type of workmanship have been found with a manufacturer's name on it.

Stove-top coffee-bean roasters that followed the early roasters had an arm and a crank that moved the beans about as they roasted. The roaster was set inside the stove hole, down close to the coals. This is shown by the extension of the body of the holder. The body of the roaster is of thin sheet iron, while the cover is of tin. One of the two roasters pictured has a short handle of sheet iron thrust into a wooden handle, while the other has a longer wire handle, with a wooden tip. The openings where the beans were poured in have small covers, one sliding out sidewise and one lifting on a hinge. One roaster would have held about one pound of beans, while the other could have taken two pounds.

Standing on the hearth in readiness was a tin foot stove. These were probably used only in the northern climes where the winters were long and severe. The stoves stood ready to be filled with hot embers or charcoal and then taken out to the sleighs. Many different sizes and shapes of foot stoves were made by the handy man of the house or by a tinsmith and wood turner.

The earliest ones appear to have been made entirely of wood. One of this type in the museum was found in Salem. It is six inches high, eight inches square, and has a door that lifts up, sliding in a groove. Holes were bored with a gimlet in all four sides and the top for draft, so that gases might escape from the burning embers or charcoal. The tin cup that held the embers was fastened to a sheet of tin, and a second

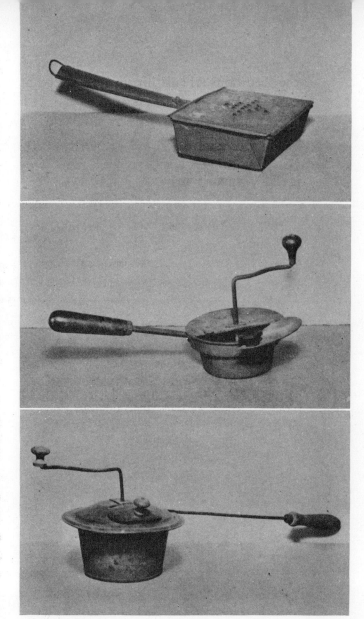

PLATES 28, 29 & 30. *When stoves came into common use new types of kitchen utensils were devised for use on the stove top. Shown here are three stove-top coffee-bean roasters. The two on the bottom were set into the stove hole.*

sheet was put on the floor for protection against overheating the wood. Some cups were round and some were square, some with a lip and some without.

The more common foot stove was the one made with pierced sheets of tin. The earliest

PLATES 31 & 32. *Foot stoves were a great help in the colder regions. The earliest types (shown on the right) were made entirely of wood except for the fire holder, but were soon replaced by those made like tin boxes (shown on the left).*

type had no frame, a six-sided box of tin, eight inches square and five and one-half inches high, with tin reinforcement on the bottom. Each sheet was cut alike and fastened to the other sheet at the edges by bending over to make a seam, or sometimes by soldering together. The top and the bottom were turned over at the edges onto the bent-up lower edges of the sides. The edges of the tin door were folded over a wire with two small openings left on one side for the hinges. Two small square hinges were soldered to one edge of the box, and these were bent over the upright wire of the door. The latch is merely a piece of wire set through a hole, twisted into a loop for

the handle and spread like a cotter pin for the catch.

The pierced design is a circle of holes, then a circle of holes and hearts, and then a circle of holes with a cross in the center. Heart designs appear to have been characteristic of Pennsylvania, but this foot stove was found in the old town of Groton, Massachusetts. Why would it not be possible for a tinsmith to copy a design that took his fancy, regardless of where he lived? Or perhaps this stove travelled with the family when it came East.

It is said that Paul Revere had a brass and iron factory in Boston in the middle of the eighteenth century, and many trays and other

PLATE 33. *Foot stoves were later made with wooden frames. Shown here are two with their respective holders for charcoal, one square, one round.*

tin-plated ironware have been accredited to him. Perhaps this gives an approximate time of the pierced tinware that rapidly found its way into the homes, such as foot stoves, lace-edge trays, lanterns, and graters.

The tin foot stove commonly found is the square one that was set in a wooden frame. The four posts were turned by a wood turner and the top was slatted, with a wire handle fastened to the slats. The tin box was made like the early foot stove without a frame. The four sides were perforated with a design, and probably each one of the many stoves had a different design. The foot stove in the museum has a heart pattern on all four sides, surrounded by a circle of perforations. Perhaps this was a gift to a young bride.

The process of making such a foot stove in a wooden frame was to nail the four turned posts to the bottom floor board. Then the tin stove was put inside the posts, and a slatted top was nailed onto the top of the posts. The stove could not slip out. A wire handle was fastened on the top with wire brads. Every stove had a small tin box to hold the embers or charcoal, either square or round, and in the long foot stoves the box was long and held double the amount of charcoal.

This type of framed foot stove was made in different shapes, oval, round, and square, and also in double and triple sizes. The patterns in the tin sheets, done in a variety of designs by local tinsmiths, are interesting to study. To all appearances the holes were punched with a nail when the sheet was placed on a piece of wood. On some of the sheets, the design does not come in the middle, showing the piercing was done

PLATE 34. *Some foot stoves were made large enough for two people to share on a sleigh or at the chilly meetinghouse.*

freehand. The double foot stove could be used by two people, and the one with three sections could have been used by three people, counting a small child between father and mother.

The foot stoves were filled on the hearth and taken to the sleigh. No sleigh hitched to old dobbin ever left the barn in winter without a foot stove tucked under the robes. There were trips to market, to singing school, and spelling bees, to quilting parties, to funerals and "bornings," and on Sabbath to the meetinghouse.

The meetinghouses were without heat until stoves were added around 1734. Even then the foot stoves were carried into the meeting for greater comfort. From all accounts, it was a woman's privilege to put her feet on a foot stove, for it is written that a man often took his dog to the service and put his feet on the warm body. That custom did not last long, for a law soon came to be put onto the records that no dog should be brought into the meetinghouse.

It is said that women often carried a hot potato in their muffs. And a small, tin hand warmer has been found which could have

PLATE 35. *Two very unusual warmers of tin. The one on the left, only five inches in diameter, contained a small carrier for charcoal and was probably carried inside a muff. The one on the right was heated by hot water and was, most likely, used in bed. From the collection of J. B. Newton of Amherst, Massachusetts.*

been carried in a muff. This small stove is about five inches in diameter and three inches high, all tin. It has a tiny door that swings on hinges, and it once carried a small container for charcoal. A small, shaped piece of soapstone has been found that was carried in a muff, worn smooth by use.

The pews were boxed in with high walls and had small doors that latched with a swivel button, so that the heat from the family foot stove, little as it was, should not be swept out into the aisle. Every family had its own pew for which they paid annual rent to the owner of the meetinghouse.

In my family there is a deed on a pew that belonged to my grandfather, Rufus Gould. It was written on a sheet of common paper, tinted a pale blue, seven inches wide and ten inches long, with a fancy embossed design in the upper corner. It is the kind of paper that was used as letter paper before the days of envelopes, when letters were folded and sealed with sealing wax and taken by stagecoach. The writing on the deed is very fine, perhaps written with a quill pen, and a plain round seal was glued at the bottom right-hand corner, following the date. It reads thus:

Know all men by these presents, that I, Rhoda Ruggles of Barre, in the County of Worcester and State of Massachusetts, both in my private capacity and as Administratrix of the goods and estate of Creighton Ruggles, late of Barre, deceased, in consideration of fifty five dollars, paid by Rufus Gould of said Barre, the receipt wherof is hereby acknowledged, do hereby give, grant, sell and convey unto the said Gould, his heirs and Assigns a certain pew situated in the Methodist Episcopal Church in said Barre, being pew number ("45") forty five.

To have and to hold the same to the said Gould, his heirs and Assigns, to his and their use and behoof forever with all privileges and appertenances thereof belonging.

And I do for myself, my heir, Executors and Administrators covenant with the said Gould, his heirs and Assigns, that I have good right to sell and convey the said premises to the said Gould and that I will and my heirs shall warrant and defend the same premises to said Gould, his heirs and Assigns, forever against unlawful claims and demands of all persons. In witness thereof I, the said Rhoda H. Ruggles in my individual capacity and as Administratrix aforesaid, have hereto set my hand and seal this fourth day of April in the year Eighteen hundred and sixty two.

Executed in my presence
G. Twichell

Rhoda H. Ruggles

In the very early days, people were seated according to their rank and according to the amount they gave to the church; those of high rank and the generous givers near the front, the less important ones next, and the common rank and file at the back. The unmarried men sat on one side, and the unmarried women on the opposite side. Boys sat on the steps leading to the high pulpit and on the gallery steps. Little girls are not mentioned, so it would seem that they never became unruly!

When stoves were put into the meeting-house, a practice that started around 1734, the seating was arranged according to the distance from the stove. Those of high rank and those who gave more money were placed next to the stove, and those of less importance farther away from the stove. Foot stoves continued to be used to the end of the nineteenth century.

One of the most conspicuous men during the service was the tithing man. He had a stick with strips of leather, sometimes knotted, attached on one end and a hare's foot or foxtail on the other. The knotted thongs were for the unruly boys, administered after service. But the foxtail at the other end was used the most. Because of the monotonous service, people had to make an effort to keep awake. If anyone was seen to nod, he or she was immediately touched with the foxtail and made alert again, per-

PLATE 37. *These are songbooks that were used in the middle of the nineteenth century in Boston and Worcester. In the author's collection.*

haps to nod again more than once thereafter. Caraway seed was supposed to help anyone to keep awake, and women often wore a bouquet of flowers with this seed in it.

The service lasted the entire Sabbath Day, with prayers, scripture reading, and singing. Prayers more often than not were an hour in length. At noontime came the recess, and the families gathered outside, sometimes in a nearby tavern for warmth and warm drinks, or in the fireroom built out in the end section of the shed for the horses, that had a fireplace in it. This recess was the lunch hour and most of the families brought their lunches to sustain themselves for a second ordeal in the afternoon. The afternoon's routine was similar to that of the morning, with prayers and exhortations.

PLATE 36. *Unruly children at church were kept in good behavior by the tithing man who, if necessary, brandished this imposing weapon with leather thongs.*

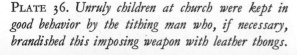
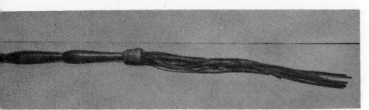

PLATE 38. *A beautiful alms box. It has a hasp for a padlock. Coins were dropped in the slot in the cover.*

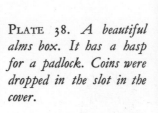

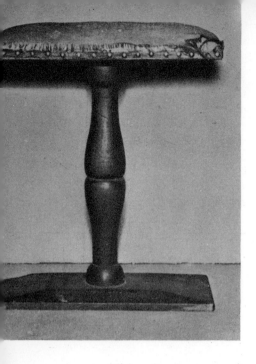

PLATE 39. *An odd relic from the days of the day-long church services is the armrest. This example is found in the Historical Society of New Braintree, Massachusetts.*

twenty-five miles northwest of Worcester, is an odd relic of the early church services, now housed in the Historical Society. It is an armrest made by one Samuel Harrington for his wife Saphrona Converse, whom he married September 19th, 1820. The rest stands fifteen inches high, a base, an upright, and an oblong top, padded with cotton and covered with a piece of homespun linen. Imagine the comfort of leaning on such an armrest in those straight-back pews! Once, there must have been many such contrivances among the various families, but long since burned as kindling wood.

For lighting in the meetinghouse, there were various holders for fish oil, whale oil, or candles. Because most of the first settlements were near the seacoast, fish oils were easily obtained and lighting equipment consisted of vessels of iron, tin, or glass filled with oil and burning tow wicks. But as soon as domestic animals could be slaughtered, tallow from fat could be had, and it was then that the tinsmith made many types of lamps, candleholders, and sconces. A later chapter will explain the progress of lighting methods.

In my museum is a pair of tin sconces that once hung in the Allen Congregational Church in Dedham, Massachusetts, twenty

This day-long service was continued in many sections until the nineteenth century.

It was during the noontime recess that the foot stoves were replenished with fresh charcoal. A friend of our family living in a nearby town told of her father as a young boy filling the foot stoves every Sabbath noon. This was more than one hundred years ago. No foot stove was forgotten. And, furthermore, if any foot stoves were left behind after the service was over, the sexton took them to his home. The owners would have to go after them and pay a "proper fine for their negligence."

In the little town of New Braintree,

PLATE 40. *Before the advent of lamps, tin sconces were made to provide light in the churches and meetinghouses. These two shown here were used in the early nineteenth century in the Allen Congregational Church in Dedham, Massachusetts.*

PLATE 41. *An ingenious candleholder was devised to hang on the back of a pew. The two pegs jutting out in the back kept the candle upright, preventing the candle from tilting because of the slant of the back of the pew.*

PLATE 42. *Some foot warmers were quite elaborate. This foot warmer was covered with ingrain carpeting, fastened to the edges with brass tacks, and was carried by a heavy cord on top.*

miles from Boston, in 1820. They are typical of that time, long and narrow, with a fluted top and a rim at the bottom to hold the drippings. Many of these were decorated in color, done at the time when painted tinware was popular. The sconces hung on either side of the high pulpit, up in the choir loft, and on the side walls.

A rare little holder for a candle came to me as a gift. It is merely a block of wood, four inches square, with a hole bored in the top for a candle. A wire extends up from the back, bent like a large hook. The holder hung by the hook on the back of a pew in front of the owner, giving the family a ray of light when the day darkened and night came on. The fact that the backs of the pews slanted was taken into consideration and

two small pegs extending about one and one-half inches were driven in near the bottom of the block. These pegs held the candle in an upright position, a simple but ingenious device.

If a collector once notices foot stoves and warming devices, he will find an interesting group with much variety. One of the last of the foot stoves to disappear was the one of tin that burned compressed cakes of charcoal. This warmer is long and narrow with a slanting top like a natural footrest. One in the museum is covered with a piece of ingrain carpeting, as good as new, fastened to the edge with brass tacks. There is a strap of heavy cord by which the warmer was carried. Within is a drawer which pulls out by a knob in the shape of a star to match the star-shaped holes in the side of the warmer, cut for vents. Stars were used as a symbol of religion. The drawer, too, has vents, both for draft and to allow the fumes of the smoldering charcoal to escape. The cake of charcoal is like a brick, long and thin, stamped LEHMAN, the name of the manufacturer. The museum boasts of a package of such cakes, bought at an auction. The cakes were considered worthless until the collection of foot stoves and foot warmers

PLATE 43. *Foot warmers made for use on sleighs. The one on the right, made of copper, was heated by hot water. The one on the left used oblong blocks of charcoal for fuel.*

began to be an important group. This carpeted warmer saw long service, taken regularly in the sleigh under the robes, to the meetinghouse on Sabbath Day and to prayer meeting. It belonged to a Worcester family and was laid away as of no value when the grandmother who had customarily used it died, and the churches no longer needed the extra heat from foot stoves.

Because soapstone was found in profusion in the common clay pits, it was used for many purposes. It was used for bases of flatirons, for mortars, for underground pipes, for muffin pans, for inkwells, for rests for the coffeepot and the teapot, and for foot warmers. It was a common thing for every family to have a slab of soapstone, with a wire handle inserted in one side, ready to be used as a foot warmer. Warmed in the embers or in the oven of a stove, the soapstone held the heat for many hours. It made a good bedfellow on a cold winter's night. In the old country, it has been said, another easily obtained bedfellow was a cotton bag filled with coarse rye meal, first heated in

PLATE 46. *The common soapstone was used for flatirons, mortars, and griddles, as well as for foot warmers. The small slab on the right was used inside a muff. Note how it has been worn down and polished by much usage over the years.*

the oven. Often several bags were put into a bed at night or in the day for a sick patient.

The soapstone foot warmer was taken in a sleigh under the robes and carried to the meetinghouse. If a family could not afford a tin foot stove heated by charcoal, it could afford a slab of soapstone. Some ingenious man thought out a holder for the slab, made of wood. The top has slats, so the heat rose to the feet resting on it. The holder illustrated has a hook that held the slab in place. Part of the fun of collecting antiques lies in finding these odd homemade things.

A very unusual foot warmer of tin is the one illustrated, owned by Nina Fletcher Little of Boston. It has a curved front with a slanting platform, and the back is three-sided, each side with a curved opening with glass windows. The tin platform lifts out by a small ring and within is a square tin lamp with one burner, which held either fish oil or whale oil. The lamp sets under a tin plate to keep it in position. There is a small opening on either side of the warmer covered with fine mesh wire, through which a draft might penetrate and from which

PLATES 44 & 45. *Front and back views of a combination foot warmer and lantern, showing the little whale-oil burner that was used both for light and heat. This piece comes from the collection of Mrs. Nina Fletcher Little of Boston.*

Antique Tin & Tole Ware ❦| 32 |❧

fumes might escape. The feet rested on the tin platform.

From the back of this foot stove, the lamp is visible through the windows and the rays from it made it possible to use the warmer as a lantern, carried by its handle in the dusk or in the evening. Leaving the sleigh and going to singing school or to a spelling bee, the family used it as a lantern. Then after dobbin had been put into his stall, the family could easily see its way to the backdoor into the kitchen. This foot warmer might well be called a combination of warmer and lantern.

This type of foot warmer with an oil lamp was also made in wood. Its construction is similar, with a platform for the feet and the three windows at the back. There is a patent on this, showing it was made by a manufacturing company and of a later date than the warmer of tin.

Patented August 15 1865
FEET WARMER
LANTERN AND FOOT-STOOL
Manufactured by
Otis H. Weed and Company
No 31 Brattle Street Boston
Directions:
Use sperm or lard oil.
Do not allow the blaze to reach the radiator.

Another combined stove and lantern is in Old Sturbridge Village. It is made with an iron top with scalloped edges, supported by four rods on a tin bottom. The top and bottom are about seven inches square and the warmer stands about six inches high. Between the top plate and the bottom is a round holder of isinglass, within which is an oil lamp. The patent reads: "Arnold's Combination Stove and Lantern April 11

PLATES 47 & 48. *This lantern, foot-warmer combination was made of wood and was patented in 1865. Note the carpeting on the footrest.*

1854." It was used as a stove on which to warm milk or other drinks, with a small lid that could be removed when the lamp was lighted, and it was also a lantern when carried by the wire handle.

A round, oil-burning foot warmer of iron was found in Salem. It has a slanting head, covered with ingrain carpeting. Under the carpeting is a sheet of tin through which the heat could penetrate to the feet resting on the slant. The head opens on a hinge, and inside is a tin lamp with two burners. The warmer was japanned and has a beautiful design of roses and leaves, in color, at the back. The head locks with a swivel turn, and at one time there was a red cord strung through ring extensions on either side, by which the warmer could be carried.

In Belchertown, Massachusetts, in the

Historical Society's Stone House, is a long tin warmer, which could have been used in an office, a store, or any room. It apparently is not a foot stove but a heater. It measures twenty inches long and eight inches wide and has perforations in the top and sides, through which the heat radiated. A long box of charcoal would have provided the heat.

Another variety of tin foot warmer was made to hold hot water for the source of heat. One oval warmer is about a foot long

PLATE 52. *This long heater in the Stone House of the Historical Society of Belchertown, Massachusetts is twenty inches long and was probably used just as a heater rather than a foot warmer.*

PLATES 49, 50 & 51. *Three views of a sturdy foot warmer made of iron and japanned with a beautiful design in color. The slanting round top is made of a sheet of tin covered with ingrain carpeting and transmitted the heat from the small oil burner in the base.*

and two inches high, with a flat top and bottom and a screw cap. Boiling water could be poured into such warmers and probably they were used for the feet in a sleigh as well as being taken to bed. There is part of a label on one, but it is illegible.

A parlor footrest-warmer that from all appearances seems to have come from France, where they were known as *chaufferettes,* is the one with a box frame of black walnut, resting on four ball feet. Over the top is fastened a choice bit of fabric with a center design of French origin. The box resembles the sewing boxes so popular at that time that held a tray and had a mirror fastened to the inside of the cover. The tin container inside the footrest is oblong to fit the frame and this has a screw cap. This was a decorative parlor piece, an attractive addition to the family's possessions, used for milady's feet, as late as the end of the nineteenth century.

Another oddity, although not of tin, is the foot muff. This was found in the same home where the French box and the tiny holder that was carried in a muff were found. The foot muff was made of leopardskin, top and sides bound with red leather like a round, flat pillow. The muff is lined with bearskin. A leather loop provides a handle by which the muff could be carried from room to room. Milady slipped her high, black laced boots into the warm fur and she avoided suffering from cold feet as she sat before a Franklin stove, probably with a handsome imported shawl over her shoulders. This fur muff, which was often found in the well appointed French parlor of the late nineteenth century, was called a *chance-lière*.

Warming pans were fashioned many years ago in the old countries. There are beautiful ones of copper and brass, with long handles and large heads, lined with tin to hold the live coals. The covers of these are very ornamental, with etched designs and a pattern of pierced holes. Few pans had the same design, each being the individual work of an artist who expressed his artistic talent in the decorations. There is a ring in the cover by which to open the head, and a six inch handle was riveted to the back.

PLATE 53. *To take the chill out of the bed, warming pans were fashioned from tin plate. Much lighter than those of brass, they were a welcome addition to the stock of household utensils.*

Into this short handle a long wooden handle was inserted. The earliest warming pans have a long iron handle, about two and one-half feet in length, with a curlycue tip by which it could be hung by the chimney. Following

PLATE 55. *For the well-appointed Victorian parlor elegant foot warmers like this one that came from France were devised. They were known as* chaufferettes. *From the Hosmer collection of Lancaster, Massachusetts.*

PLATE 54. *An unusual piece of French extraction is this leopardskin foot muff known as a* chance-lière. *It is lined with bearskin.*

Tin on the Hearth

PLATE 56. *Among the many things that were made of tin in the early days was this pipe rack which hung by the chimney. A fresh supply of tobacco was kept in the container in its base. From the Historical Society of Belchertown, Massachusetts.*

the iron handle came the wooden handle, turned on the lathe by a wood turner, long and with a shaped tip. The pan was filled with live coals from the fireplace and thrust between the homespun sheets and moved back and forth, to take off the chill. Seldom was there heat in a bedroom, which fact made a warm bed more comfortable. These copper and brass warming pans are prized by many a family today and they still lean against a chimney breast, often in an old home that has been restored.

When tin appeared in the beginning of the nineteenth century as a material for household equipment and when the tinsmith began his work, a tin warming pan was fashioned. The one in the museum was the first piece that started the collection of tin along the earlier collections of wood and iron. It has a head of two shaped-plates,

soldered together, with a screw cap in a sunken center. A handle thirty-two inches long was made of three tubular sections soldered together and soldered to the head in a cone-shaped piece of tin. This tin warming pan is very light in weight and it must have been far easier than those of brass to swing back and forth in a bed. There might have been a disadvantage in using hot water in that it did not retain its heat as long as live coals. This tin warmer was patented in 1882 by E. M. Ames.

A second tin warming pan was found and this has a short handle. It was made with two deep plates soldered to a band of tin, with a protruding snout which was sealed with a cork. The handle is only a foot long, closed at the end, with a ring by which the pan was hung when not in use. Perhaps this short-handled pan remained in bed with the sleeper and continued to give comfort as long as the water remained warm. This has no patent on it and was presumably the work of a local tinsmith.

An interesting find was a clay-pipe holder of tin which hung by the chimney. The upper rack holds six clay pipes, the stems stuck into holes with the bowls showing above the rack. Below this rack is a box with a lid where the tobacco was kept, in readiness for filling the pipes, sometimes corncob pipes. The rack measures about ten inches long and eight inches wide.

CHAPTER THREE

Household Utensils of Tin

THE HOUSEHOLD utensils and contrivances that were in use in the home between 1750 and 1890 were many and it would be impossible to describe them all. One gadget after another was made by local blacksmiths or tinsmiths and later by manufacturers who sprang up as demands for tinware increased, each locality thinking up something useful and something different.

A tinsmith was one who worked in tin and tin plate, called often a tinner. A tinsmith was also called a whitesmith, for it was a whitesmith who finished and polished ironwork. Since tin utensils were made from tin plate, or thin sheets of iron covered with a thin coating of tin, they needed finishing and polishing after they were made. A tinsmith sold his wares from house to house as a peddler, sometimes on foot, sometimes on a horse, and in later years he used a cart or wagon. A later chapter tells of peddlers and the tin peddler's cart.

After these tin utensils were made, they had to be kept in repair. It was then that the tinker came into existence. The *Century Dictionary* says that a "tinker was the lowest order of craftsmen and their occupation was often pursued, especially by gypsies, as a mere cover for vagabondage." The name tinker comes from the word "tink," which described the sound of the beating on a tin pan which the tinker used to make known his approach. Anyone wandering in the streets with no occupation was called a tramp, and the town officers accosted such men and put them in the town lockup. Most country towns had lockups or jails. The small lockup, called a "tramp house," was made of brick and consisted of one cell with a door and two small windows set in near the roof. Such a lockup is still seen in a few small country towns, usually not far from the church, the horse sheds, and the town hall. Jails were classified as buildings and were generally built of brick. An odd arrangement found in Newfane, Vermont, home of Eugene Field, the poet, is a jail built as an addition to the town inn. It is strange to see the sunny, broad piazza of

PLATES 57 & 58. *The itinerant tinker carried his tools in containers like this, known as the "tinker's pig." From the collection of Mrs. G.W.B. Bailey of Harriman, New York.*

the inn and the barred windows of the jail next to each other.

So in the early years, the tinker, regarded as one of the lowest order of craftsmen, went from house to house mending tinware. He carried his tools and mended any and all household utensils of tin, brass, and copper such as kettles, pans, churns, teakettles, and other small wares. He carried solder and clay. When a seam or hole needed mending, he made a clay dam around the part to be mended. Molten solder was poured into the dam, and the seam or hole was mended with a hot iron tool. The clay could be used over again, but it was usually thrown away as worthless. It is from this fact that the expression, "I don't give a tinker's dam," has been derived, conveying a lack of concern over the matter at hand. Polite society might say, "I don't care a rap!"

From the position of a semi-vagabond, the tinker rose to a position of an expert and, in cooperation with the tinsmith, he became an important man in his community. He carried a tin holder for his tools, solder, and clay, made much like the rounded candleboxes and specimen boxes of the day, sometimes with small additional holders at the ends of the box. This long holder was slung over the tinker's shoulder with a

leather strap as he made his journeys. The holder was called the tinker's pig, a name coined from the appearance of the earliest types of these holders. The long tubular body had four short, bracket legs, a handle at one end that looked like a tail, and a snout-shaped addition at the other end. This pointed addition was made to accomodate the longer tools. A door, made like the door of the tin kitchen, dropped down on hinges. This early tinker's pig could be carried by the handle, hanging by the tinker's side, as well as by a strap over the shoulder. One such holder is in Old Sturbridge Village.

Another tinker's pig is illustrated, loaned to me to photograph by Mrs. Gillian W. B. Bailey of Harriman, New York, a collector of rare pieces of tin. This has a body about twenty inches long and at either end is a small container added for small tools. This pig was carried by means of a cord fastened to rings at either end of the body, the cord slung over the tinker's shoulder. The group of tools in another illustration must have had technical names, but for an amateur, they are merely tools.

Like all peddlers and itinerants, the tinker remained in a locality for a day, or possibly for several days, receiving his "keep" while working. And of course he brought the latest news from the "outside," and as he moved on his stock of information was forever increasing. A sign that used to hang in Buckthorn Inn of New York City between 1800 and 1820 shows how the tinker was ranked:

Fourpence a night for a bed
Sixpence with supper
No more than five to sleep in one bed
No boots to be worn in bed
Organ grinders to sleep in the washhouse
No dogs allowed upstairs
No beer allowed in the kitchen
No razor grinders or Tinkers taken

The first two pieces of tinware that I bought were a tin grater and a sausage gun, which is a tin holder with a wooden plunger. I went to an auction not many miles from Worcester when I was collecting woodenware. I was a novice at collecting in those first years beginning in 1934 and I had had little experience with auctions. But anything unusual fascinated me. At that auction,

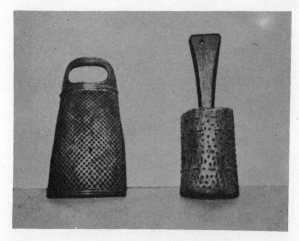

PLATE 60. *Two tin graters from different periods. The one on the right is a very early handmade model.*

I remember bringing home two stools such as cobblers used for thirty-five cents; a beautiful etching of Beethoven in a large golden frame with a wide rim for two seventy-five—my profession had been music for many years; two crane hooks for fifty cents; and an odd lot that contained a wooden spoon, two graters, and a sausage gun for one sixty-five. It was the spoon that I wanted, but it was lumped in with the other three pieces, which I had to take. The graters and the sausage gun did not interest me then, but in the course of time I found they were important additions to a collection of woodenware. Inscribed on the back of the grater were the initials "A F" and the date 1794. I knew the Forbes family that had once owned it. Any mark on a piece that gives some history is appreciated by collectors.

Those early tin graters were made by cutting a piece of wood in the shape of a long thin block with an extending handle. A shaped piece of tin was then pierced with holes by laying it on a board and pounding

PLATE 59. *These were the elementary tools that were used by tinkers as they made their way from community to community, repairing tin goods.*

Household Utensils of Tin

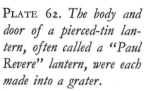

PLATE 61. *An assortment of early graters showing the differences in sizes and styles. The one in the center was also used as a strainer.*

PLATE 62. *The body and door of a pierced-tin lantern, often called a "Paul Revere" lantern, were each made into a grater.*

a nail into it to make the perforations. Then this sheet was curved and nailed to the sides of the block, with a space left between the sheet and the block. The rough side of the tin was the outside, the sharp points making the grater.

The many graters of that time had different patterns pierced in the tin. Some are quite artistic with dots and dashes, some with rows of dashes, and others with circles. I have two graters that would delight any collector. They were made from an old lantern, often erroneously called a Paul Revere lantern. The door and the conical top of the lantern were taken off. A shaped slab of wood was fitted into the space where the door had been, the handle extending four or five inches. This made one grater. The door itself was nailed onto a slab of wood which has a knob handle, which made a second grater. Both pieces have a pattern of a star cut in gashes, one large star in the lantern and two smaller ones in the door, a typical pattern on many tin lanterns.

I found this lantern grater in a barnshop near Worcester. The larger piece was on a

fifty-cent table, and I was not particularly impressed with it after I had paid my money. As I was going down the rickety stairs from the barn loft, my eyes fell on something hanging from an overhead beam. It was another grater that cost another fifty cents. All the way home, my mind kept seeing the patterns on the two pieces and I tried to figure out what relation they had to each other. When I arrived home and examined them again, I saw that the two pieces had once been one lantern. The places where the hinges and the latch had been showed on each grater.

There was another kind of grater that was a combination of grater and strainer. One such piece was made like a sturdy wooden box with a tin bottom. The tin has small slits, so the under part could have been used as a grater and the box as a strainer or colander. A small framed piece of tin also made a hand grater and small strainer.

To show what Yankee ingenuity could do, there is nothing in the museum more expressive than an old chopping bowl. The bottom of the bowl had worn through over the years, making it useless. Someone in the family—perhaps a grandpa—cut the entire bottom out, making a large oblong hole. On the inside of this, a sheet of tin was nailed with crude handmade nails. This made a sizable colander and the under part could have been used as a grater. The old bowl gave out again when cracks developed on both ends. Again, grandpa was called upon, or perhaps a younger generation had grown up as the years had passed and was asked to do the job. Two strips of iron were riveted across the split ends. Once more the strainer-grater could be kept in use.

One grater measures fifteen inches long, and the question came up as to why it was made such a size. The job of grating raw potatoes was no easy task, and perhaps the idea was that with a larger grater and a potato in each hand, the job could have been done more quickly.

A cookbook in our family belonged to my grandmother, Mary Henry Gould, called the *New England Housekeeper,* dated 1845. A rule for potato starch says: "Peel and grate a quantity of potatoes; put pulp into

PLATE 64. *After a chopping bowl had worn through, it was converted into a strainer by cutting the bottom out and attaching a sheet of pierced tin in its place.*

a coarse cloth between two boards, and press it into a dry cake; the juice thus pressed out of the pulp must be mixed with an equal quantity of water, and in an hour's time, it will deposit a fine sediment on which pour boiling water and your starch is ready for use."

Potatoes were also used in liquid yeast. In the same cookbook of my grandmother's is a simple rule: "make a fresh batch of yeast for every new baking." Imagine making the yeast before the bread could be made! But with the bread baked in those brick ovens, it must have been something worth working for. "Five large potatoes boiled and mashed, three pints of boiling water, flour enough to make it a little thicker than flap-jacks, and one cup of yeast. This is enough to rise five loaves of bread, which may be mixed with water or milk,

PLATE 63. *Sturdy strainers like these were also used as graters by the early settlers.*

and will rise enough while your oven is heating. Save enough of the yeast for your next baking." The cup of yeast mentioned was old, kept in a jar on the kitchen shelf, and was passed down in the family through the years or at times even loaned to a neighbor. The box graters and the converted chopping bowl were doubtless used as colanders for starch and yeast.

For a long time butter was colored with the juice of carrots. The carrots were grated on tin graters and then simmered in water. The juice was strained in colanders. During the heat of the summer, cow's milk was whiter than at any other time. To offset this, the butter made then was colored with carrot juice. Poor butter as well could be colored and made to appear of the best quality. The custom of coloring butter

PLATE 67. *Nutmegs were imported from the West Indies and used extensively in the early households. The preserved nutmegs in the center were brought home on a whaling vessel over one hundred and fifty years ago. The grater on the left is dated 1740.*

PLATES 65 & 66. *Shown here are two spice boxes each with eight small containers. The earlier model on top is made of wood with rims of tin. The bottom box is made of tin and is japanned with gold lines.*

became a common practice and a law was enacted forbidding this deceptive practice.

Tin graters for nutmegs are numerous, some of them still in use today. Perhaps there is more romance in using the grandmother's grater and a whole nutmeg than there is in sprinkling powdered nutmeg from a tin can! The families loved pies in the old days even more than they do now, and it was a common thing to serve pie even for breakfast.

The nutmeg was brought from the West Indies; preserving and pickling called for spices of all sorts. The nutmeg grew in a hard shell that was shaped like a peach. Around the nutmeg inside the shell was a lacy covering called mace. The outer shell was removed and thrown away, the lacy covering, or the mace, was next removed, and then both the mace and the nutmeg were laid away to dry in spice boxes. These were first made of wood and later of tin. Before they could be used, the mace was powdered in a mortar with a pestle, and the nutmeg was grated. In many graters there is a holder that held the nutmeg against the grating plate, and the holder was rubbed back and forth. Or, as in some graters, the nutmeg was forced against the grater by turning a crank.

The large cylindrical can in the illustration was a combination of flour holder with a sprinkler top, a cooky cutter at the bottom, and a grater on one side. A small compartment was made in the cylinder for keeping the nutmeg. In Old Sturbridge Village there is a similar tin combination device with a tin pastry jigger attached to one side.

An interesting little grater is the one scarcely two inches long. On one side is a cover that lifts and inside is a nutmeg. The grater is on the opposite side. When a man went to see a neighbor and drinks were made in the tankard and served in front of the blazing logs, the little nutmeg grater went along, too, tucked into the vest pocket. Then the visitor could flavor his own drink to suit himself, perhaps even sharing his nutmeg. This rare grater was in the home where the apple roaster discussed in the previous chapter had been, and it can easily be said that the grater is well over one hundred years old. In that home, the birthplace of one of my schoolmates, everything had been labelled and dated, giving much history for others to read.

In old England, the small graters were called nutmeg boxes. They were made of silver, Battersea enamel, wood, Sheffield plate, iron, brass, and ivory. They were used "in the days when every gentleman thought himself a dab at brewing a bowl of punch."*

* Sir James Yoxall.

The tin sausage gun was an early implement. These guns were made in various lengths and had a plunger of wood. They were used in making sausages, or "hog's puddings" as they were called in the early days. In my family's old cookbook of 1845, the rule for sausage meat was: "Take the piece of pork designed for sausages and chop it up, and if it is too fat, add a little lean beef; season with sage or summer savory, salt and pepper; then fry a small piece to see if it is seasoned right. If you prefer not to stuff them into skins, you may take pieces of cotton cloth, eight or nine inches wide, and two or three feet long, and sew the sides together and at one end; then wet it and stuff your meat in as solid as you can and hang them up in a cool dry place. It will keep as well or better than in skins; when used, peel the cloth down no farther than you slice off."

Another kind of sausage stuffer was found upcountry. It consists of twelve tin tubes, each a foot long and two inches in

PLATE 68. *An assortment of small nutmeg graters are shown. The can on the left is a combination grater and flour holder that could also be used as a cooky cutter. The diminutive one in the front was carried in the vest pocket for flavoring drinks when visiting.*

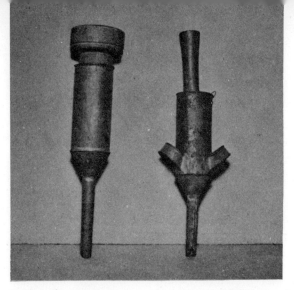

PLATE 69. *Homemade sausages were stuffed by hand with sausage guns like these two shown here.*

diameter. These stand upright in a red, wooden box, divided into twelve sections. With them was a long stick, a little less than the diameter of the tubes, with a knob handle. This was the stuffer. No one could describe the operation to me, but the process must have been to chop and season the meat and stuff it into these tubes, instead of the cotton cloth bags. The tubes would have had to be well greased so that the long filling of meat could have slid out when needed, one tube at a time. Then the meat would have been sliced and fried as sausage cakes. Cakes came before sausage links and were first called hog's pudding or blood pudding if mixed with the blood of the hog.

The commonly found sausage gun consists of a tubular piece of tin, with a snout on one end and a small ring at the other by which it was hung. The wooden plunger often went astray and was used as a potato masher, a pestle in a mortar, and even as a hammer to pound with. They were shaped to fit the gun snugly, and the heads were molded to provide a good grip when the

meat was pushed into the gun. Stretching our imagination to the utmost, we cannot think of modern generations going through the ordeal of using muscle and brains to stuff a sausage gun.

The outside layer of the intestine of a hog was used as a casing, cut into lengths of two yards each. The intestine was turned inside out, scraped well, then put into salt and water to soak until used. One end was slipped onto the snout of the gun, and the chopped-pork mixture was pushed through into the skin. The link was tied in sections, of no definite lengths, sometimes just ball size. For a meal, the links were boiled or fried and placed on clean straw when taken from the kettle, the straw absorbing the grease. These sausages, known then as puddings, were served as a main dish or used to garnish fowls and hash. At that time, the diaries read, "Arrived at pudding time," meaning at the first course of the meal, rather than at the end of a meal as later generations would have interpreted the expression.

PLATE 70. *Another rather unusual device for making sausages was this set of tin sausage holders, which were stuffed with the wooden stuffer shown.*

PLATE 72. *This sausage gun was rigged to an ingeniously contrived wooden box. The plunger was fastened to the wheel, which made the task of pumping the meat into the sausage gun much easier.*

were being stuffed. There is a slender gun four feet long, with a pestle the length of the gun, made of hickory. This came from a tavern in New Hampshire and one can well imagine the number of sausages that came out of a four-foot-long gun in one operation.

PLATE 71. *In the busy tavern the small sausage guns could not keep up with the demand, and large sausage guns like the four-foot long one shown here were made.*

To chop the meat would have been no small task. A collection of seventy handmade chopping knives such as are in my museum show the ingenuity of the handy man or the village smithy. No two are alike. The latest addition was the one with a short handle that was set crosswise to the blade —there could not have been many of its kind, for I was on the lookout for them for twelve years before I found this particular example.

As in all household tools, many localities produced guns that showed variations from those produced in other areas. One man rigged his gun in a box with the wooden plunger fastened to a wheel that pumped the meat into the gun. Another contrived an affair with cranks. These alleviated the task of holding the gun while the skins

Some chopping bowls were made long and narrow, some only the width of the

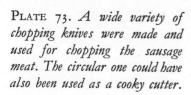

PLATE 73. *A wide variety of chopping knives were made and used for chopping the sausage meat. The circular one could have also been used as a cooky cutter.*

45 *Household Utensils of Tin*

chopping knife, others round. Hand-hewn bowls are much sought after, especially those made from the wart of the maple, called a burl.

In a barnshop in New Hampshire, a dealer had discarded what he called a piece of junk. It was a sausage gun on a platform with four long, slender legs. The plunger was fastened to a long arm pegged to an upright at one end. The snout of the gun extended below the platform so the intestine that was being filled could have been in a tub underneath the platform.

Not long after the platform gun was brought home, while I was still enthusiastic about its fine workmanship, I was asked into a home upcountry not far from Worcester to see "something queer with a long handle." The "something queer" was a platform, fulcrum, and arm for a sausage gun. The plunger was still on the arm but the gun was missing—taken out to be

PLATE 75. *Another set of chopping knives showing the diversity in design. The double-bladed one with the crossed blades is very rare.*

washed and never returned, perhaps. This piece had no legs but was used resting on a table and a high stool or on the backs of two chairs. Somehow, when your mind is searching for facts about certain things, and you are trying to put your patchwork of information together, there is always another opening for you, not too far away. If you are a real collector, you never give up the idea of finding the piece under search.

Tin meat-loaf pressers followed the days of making sausages with meat guns. A story is told here in Worcester of a certain woman who, many years ago, made delicious sausage meat pressed into loaves and peddled it, first in the neighborhood and later about the entire town. She had it in packages of one pound and two pounds, and her customers were numerous.

One meat-loaf presser has the following label: *"Man'f'ed by Sanders and Clark 85 Salem Street Worcester Mass."* The presser has a tin box eight inches square and about six inches deep, which rests on a board with two uprights. Fastened to the upright arms is an iron crossbar, into which fits a threaded rod with a wheel handle. The meat to be pressed was put into the pan, a thin square board and an iron plate placed on it, and the

PLATE 74. *This sausage gun, mounted on a four-legged platform, with the plunger attached to the long handle, was a great improvement over earlier types.*

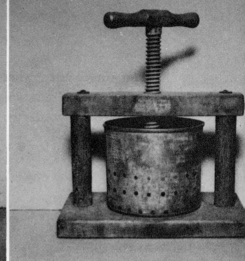

PLATES 77 & 78. *Meat-loaf pressers like the one shown on the left were developed after the sausage guns. The meat was pressed and left overnight before being served as meat loaf. On the right is shown a wine press used for extracting juices from grapes and elderberries.*

screw arm adjusted above it. As the screw pressed the plate down, the meat was pressed and shaped. This was left overnight in the press, to be served the following day. Many were the varieties of making a meat loaf.

A similar press is the one used for extracting juice from grapes and elderberries for wine. This has a round, tin holder set in a wooden frame which has a wooden screw set into the top crossbar. At the base of the holder are three rows of holes through which the juice oozed out. Cut into the floor board, or the drain board, is a circular groove, larger than the tin holder. An opening in the groove at the front acted

PLATE 76. *Another improved sausage gun was mounted on a board and was used with two supports.*

like a trough. This grooved board was made like the cheeseboard or a floor with a circular drain, out of which ran the whey into a tub below. The grapes were put into this wine press, a thin board placed on top of them, and the screw was screwed down, pushing on the board evenly. The juice from the fruit pulp ran into the circular drain and out into a tub which had been placed below.

In an illustration in *Early Copper, Tin and Brass* by Kauffman, a wine press or juicer has a tin basin with a snout, resting under the holder on the floor board, to catch the juices as they were squeezed out of the pulp. This would seem more sanitary and more easily done, having a basin with a pouring snout for the juice rather than letting the juice run down to the grooved board, around the circle, out the trough, and into a tub. One might think the tin basin was missing in the press in my museum, but the groove explains the working of the implement, and there never was a basin. Many were the wine presses, for wild grapes and elderberries grew in profusion. Home-made presses were easily set up, and wooden-ware factories came in due time to make the necessary utensils and implements. Most of the presses had either a tin box to hold the pulp or a tin snout out of which the juices ran.

When New Englanders think of baked beans, they think of the accompanying brown bread. These two went together as far back as the days of the brick ovens. A village bakeshop was often set up in the tavern, facing the common, and here the pots of beans were taken Saturday morning and called for that night in time for supper, with a loaf of brown bread added. Sometimes the village baker made the rounds himself and gathered the many pots that were to go into the brick oven.

Beans were known to the native Indians and to the colonists and was a staple food. The Indians baked them in earthen pots of their own making, in a fire hole. The fire hole was replaced by the brick oven, and that in turn was replaced by the stove, which today has been replaced by electric contrivances.

A rule for brown bread in the family's cookbook of 1845 reads: "Take one quart of Indian meal, and one quart of wheat meal, one quart of sour milk, half a tea-cupful of molasses, a heaping tea-spoonful of saleratus, and a little salt; stir it with a spoon, and bake it in a tin or iron basin, about two hours."

Illustrated is a round brown-bread tin.

It has a hollow center projection, and is found in other sizes. The tin with corrugations, made of two pieces held together by a wire hoop at the top was used for white bread. The corrugations were to facilitate cutting the bread into slices when it was ready to be served. Both tin holders could have been used at the time of stoves, placed in the oven or over steam on top of the stove.

Grapes were used primarily for fermented drinks. Records do not mention when grapes began to be dried and used as raisins. Nor does it say when the raisins went into brown bread. But in time, the raisins became as much a part of the bread as the bread was an adjunct to the beans.

The transition from the open fire to stoves came about slowly, because even after stoves had begun to be manufactured not every locality nor every family could have easy access to them, especially in the outlying districts. The late Frank King Swain of Fonthill, Doylestown, Pennsylvania, has told many interesting facts in his correspondence with me. His letters are invaluable records of those early days, made possible by his association with his grandmother and his desire to preserve early history. Quoting one letter in part: "My grandmother cooked on the open fire until 1868. The reason she stopped was because her son, returning

PLATES 79 & 80. *Baked beans and brown bread were a favorite meal. The round tin with a center hole was used for baking brown bread, while the long tin with the corrugations was used for white bread.*

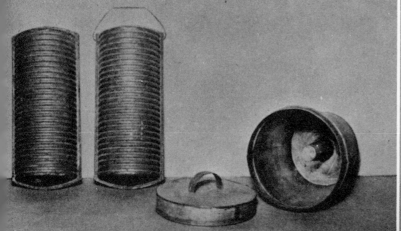

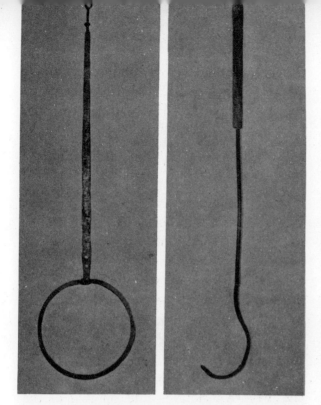

PLATES 81 & 82. *Shown here are two types of tools that were made for taking pots of beans, puddings, bread tins, etc. from the brick oven.*

from the Civil War, became engaged to a very fine lady and started to buy furnishings for his house. Of course a new cook stove was desired—a heavy cumbersome thing we would think now. He fell from a church roof while working and the old war wound was opened up and he died soon after, unmarried. So grandmother got all his belongings. And the new cook stove was a great delight to her. Her old iron vessels were too heavy but she kept them and had tinware made by the local blacksmith. This was rolled unevenly and tinned very thick and rough and never rusted. It would last forever."

The process of washing and ironing was fully explained in my book *The Early American House.* Coming under the head of tin is the patented contrivance for washing

clothes in a tub. It has a tin suction cup controlled by an iron cogwheel turned by an iron crank. The suction cup has a vent in the top for air and a frame at the bottom to prevent the clothes from being sucked in as the cup was worked up and down in the tub of clothes. This was the forerunner of suction washing; previously the idea had been merely mangling. A stick at one side held by a screw could be adjusted to the distance the cup worked most efficiently in the tub.

The washer was a rare find for me and it appears that it must be the only one of its kind, with "patent pending." After leaving a country auction one Saturday afternoon, I stopped at a shop nearby. The man had sold out everything, discontinuing his shop from necessity. "Got one piece left. You can have it for a dollar," he told me. It was the washing contrivance, lying on the floor under an empty showcase. I bought it out of curiosity. I had not the slightest idea then what it was or how it

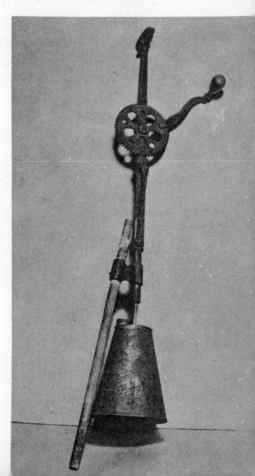

PLATE 83. *This is a unique washing contrivance that operated a suction cup with a crank. The height of the suction cup could be adjusted by the pole extending on the left.*

PLATE 84. *A simple gadget used for washing was this tin suction cup with a handle.*

worked, but it has proved a very important piece in the museum, a rare device in the history of washing.

Antique shops have been displaying a tin washer which appeared soon after 1900. It is a foot-long oblong contrivance, made like a tent, tapering at the top with an air vent, and it has two, foot-long tubular arms with a bar across the top for a handle. This has a brass plate on one side reading, "PERFECT LITTLE WASHER PATENT PENDING." It was used in a tub of clothes, rocked back and forth to mangle the clothes. That piece is still used occasionally in my family today. Another piece displayed as an "antique" is the clothes sprinkler. It is a tin can with an extending handle and a perforated screw cover. Such a handy contrivance is still doing heavy duty in our house.

When flatirons were heated on the stove top, there were many holders for them, of tin as well as of iron. The tin one in the museum was a gift. It has a cone-shaped center through which the heat rose. Three slots held three flatirons, standing on end. And as they rested against the cone, they became hot, one always ready to be changed for a cooled-off one.

A tin fluter is a clumsy affair. Gashes were cut at regular distances in a sheet of tin, twelve inches long and twelve inches wide. A small piece of tin was the tool, about six inches long, bent in two angles. The piece of cloth to be fluted or pleated was dampened, and then, beginning at the top of the tin, it was pressed into each groove with the shorter blade, the distance of the width of the blade. It was pressed into each groove the entire length of the cloth. The cloth remained until dry, then was taken out and sewn in shape as a fluted ruffle. It could not have been a very practical piece nor did it survive the years.

Ruffles and pleats were used on both men and women's clothing and on that of the children as well. They were also used on canopies of beds, both on the top, the tester, and at the bottom of the valance below the rail. The story of the costumes worn by the colonists is a fascinating one and shows how the pendulum swung back and forth, from severity to gaudiness, from gaudiness to severity.

The tin butter churn stands about two

PLATE 85. *Flatirons were heated on the stove top, and contrivances like this which held three flatirons at a time were made for greater convenience and efficiency.*

PLATE 86. *A rare find was this old milk pan containing a complete alphabet of wooden letter stamps and a paint pad.*

PLATE 87. *This simple gadget was used for making ruffles on cloth. The cloth was dampened and slid into the grooves with the narrow tin implement shown.*

feet high. The splash cup was made with the cover that sets inside the flared top, and underneath the cover is a foot-long cone soldered to the cover, all to prevent the cream from splashing out. The common churn was wooden, staved, and hooped, in many sizes and made in many styles; there were rocking churns, swinging churns, and those with a plunger or a crank. Few tin churns are found in comparison with the many of wood.

Tin milk pans usurped those of porcelain or pottery, for they were lighter in weight and did not break. Some pans were shallow and others deep. Milk was poured each day to set for cream, which was taken off with skimmers, either of wood or tin. The tin milk pan shown here was used to hold wooden letter stamps and a paint pad, a complete alphabet in the pan. These stamps were used when stamping initials or names on box covers, barrelheads, and bucket covers.

A group of tin pieces was sent to me to photograph from the museum of David Gwinn, Pennbrook Milk Company, Phila-

PLATE 88. *Most early butter churns were made of wood. Occasionally, however, they were made of tin, like this one shown here. Note the splash cup.*

Household Utensils of Tin

PLATE 89. *Later butter churns used rotating blades to churn the cream. The one on the right is a rare piece with cogwheels of bone. The cream was poured in from the opening on the wooden top.*

delphia. Mr.

outstanding collection of dairy equipment and exhibits in a wide territory, both in this country and in Canada. A rare piece among this group is the piggy churn, so called because of the snout at one end and the tail handle at the opposite end. This measures four feet long, resting on bracket feet. When making butter, the churn was suspended from the ceiling by straps which were run through two rings on the top of the churn. The worker gripped the handle and swung the churn, moving it back and

PLATE 90. *This unusual piggy churn is from the Gwinn collection of the Pennbrook Milk Co., Philadelphia. The churn was suspended from the ceiling with straps and was rocked back and forth.*

through which the air circulated. The churn has a brass label on it:

Manfactured by
Dairy Supply Company
J. Campbell's Patent
June 18, 1875

Another churn is the one with a wooden crank. Within is a set of arms which fit into the wooden gear arms of the rod leading from the crank. These meshed and thus agitated the cream. This churn was found in Chambersburg, Pennsylvania.

A rare, small churn is the one with bone gears working in a small cogwheel of bone, apparently beef bone from the farm. The fins within the tin can are tin. The part that holds the gears, the cover, uprights, and crank are all of wood. There is an opening through which the buttermilk was poured. This is claimed to have been used about 1800.

A milk container accredited to the Penn-

Antique Tin & Tole Ware ❧ 52 ❧

sylvania Dutch is of tin, with the cap fastened to the snout by a chain, preventing it from being lost. Another piece is a small tin receptacle with a wire handle and a china knob on the cover, standing about eight inches high. This was used by the wealthier families, who took it to the dairy stores or to the milk peddler and obtained their cream for home use. This was used in Baltimore, Maryland, about 1880 and was different from the ordinary tin and enamel cans that were commonly used. I am indebted to the Pennbrook Milk Company for this information.

Photographed also is the two-quart can used in our family for many years and a pint measuring-can, to measure milk or other liquids. A tall tin can with a wooden whipper belonged to a housewife, who whipped her cream with it. It is very primitive and must have been of little use because so much time would have been spent in bringing the cream to any degree of stiffness

PLATE 93. *A cream whipper, more fittingly called a cream shaker, was used for making a favorite drink called a sillabub, made with cream and wine.*

with a simple stick like the one used in this whipper.

A later cream whipper for a small amount of cream is the slender can that is about eight inches high. This tapers, and inside is

PLATES 91 & 92. *The two-quart milk can on the left that has a spout with a small lid is from the Gwinn collection and is accredited to the Pennsylvania Dutch.*

PLATE 94. *This boxlike cream whipper had rotating wire beaters. From the collection of John H. O'Connor.*

a contrivance with a revolving wheel with fanlike arms, set onto a rod at the end of which are two triangular arms. This piece is more fittingly called a cream shaker, for after the cream was poured into the cylinder, the rod with the wheel was dropped in and the container was shaken up and down, causing the wheel to spin around the rod and whip the cream. Later research showed me that the cream whipper was really fashioned to make a sillabub. That was a very popular drink. Sweetened cream and wine were whipped together or wine or cider was mixed with milk to form a soft curd. The whipper made just one drink at a time.

Another cream whipper is a boxlike container with a crank. It stands about ten inches high. Within the box is a wheel with four arms, each arm having three wires set on a slant. The wires acted as beaters for the cream. It was a family affair and could also have been used for a batch of butter.

The story of the discovery of butter is well worth mentioning, for it proves that many discoveries were accidental. The Arabs carried their milk in skin bags on the backs of camels. The rolling gait of the camel agitated the milk and butter was the result.

The pantry utensils of tin must have been a joy, for they were light in weight, shiny, and easy to keep clean. Perhaps, because of rust, they did not last as long as the wooden utensils, but the brightness brought a cheerful note into the homes. Wood had held sway for several generations, and when the blacksmith and the tinsmith and the tin peddlers made it possible to have tinware, wooden utensils, with few exceptions, became mere kindling wood. Not all woodenware became kindling wood, fortunately, for collectors have saved much from destruction, and there are many collections today. In my museum are rolling pins, pie crimpers, cooky rollers, lemon borers and lemon squeezers, scoops, skimmers, ladles, spoons, all the butter equipment, the eating equipment, and the wooden washing tools.* A trend for collecting decorative woodenware has returned and, together with the interest in old houses, kitchen utensils, and fireplace equipment, it is helping recreate the life of those pioneer generations.

An unusual find was the tin molding sheet and a tin rolling pin. Wooden molding boards and wooden rolling pins had always been used, but why was not the patented sheet of tin a more practical thing since the pastry would not stick to the tin. Mr. Swain

* Gould, *Early American Wooden Ware.*

suggested the possibility that it was used for candy, rich cookies, or puff paste, something that had to remain cold while it was being worked. But it was most likely a New England invention, practical and different, used for ordinary pastry.

The sheet is double, measuring seventeen inches wide and nineteen inches long, a smooth heavy piece of tin on the top side and a ribbed piece on the back. The ribbed or fluted back prevented the sheet from buckling or bending. The two pieces were seamed together and the ends rolled over. At one end, the sheet was turned up to make a shelf to hold the tin rolling pin. On the other end was a ring, now missing, by which the sheet was hung, the rolling pin lying in the shelf, all ready to be taken down

PLATE 96. *There are endless varieties of pie crimpers of unusual craftsmanship. These are made, respectively from left to right, of wood, of iron, and of tin.*

PLATE 95. *A rare moulding sheet of tin with a tin rolling pin. The back is made of corrugated tin.*

and used the next baking day. There was once a label on the back, but only remnants of it are left. Tin must have been a fine surface for rolling out pastry and cookies. The dough would not stick, and the sheet never needed to be floured, and it could be kept clean with little effort.

The rolling pin is a hollow cylinder of tin, beautifully seamed at the ends, measuring ten inches long. A small iron rod runs through the center onto which the wooden handles were driven. The handles and the rod revolve inside the cylinder, as do the handles on wooden rolling pins. This outfit belonged to a descendant of Simon Willard, the famous clocksmith.

Pie crimpers were used to run around the edge of the pie after the two crusts had been set together. The crimpers crimped the edge and cut off any extra dough. Pie crimpers were also used to cut around cookies, and then the tool was called a pastry jigger. Many are found in wood and are beautiful specimens of handwork. One such

PLATE 97. *Among the numerous tin utensils that were used in the kitchen were spatulas, skimmers, squeezers, maple-sugar molds, and cooky cutters of the sort shown.*

pastry jigger is of cast brass and one is of iron, both of which have a serrated end opposite the wheel, much like a pinking tool. One crimper consists of a wooden handle with a tin wheel, an inch in diameter, made of four thin sheets of tin set together with solder, which makes oval spaces that cut into the dough. Another crimper has a corrugated wooden wheel set between two tin wheels. The outer wheel extends so that when the wooden crimping wheel crimped the edges of the pie, the tin wheel cut off the extra dough.

Pies were baked in large numbers and laid away to freeze in the larder to be re-heated in the tin biscuit ovens when needed. The beginning of pies came about as a means of serving meat stews in a more tempting manner, between two crusts. It has been recorded that one pie in the lean years consisted of bear's meat served be-tween two crusts made of corn meal and water. Fruits of all descriptions went into pies, but the favorite was and still is apple pie, spelled once as it sounded, aplepye.

Tin cooky cutters were made without number. The early ones were made with fluted edges in various shapes to represent many things, such as animals, flowers, stars, crescents, hearts, diamonds, men, women, boys, and girls. A shaped, flat piece of tin for the top, a fluted cutter soldered to the under part of the rim, a shaped strip of tin soldered within the rim, and you had a cooky cutter. The favorite shape was the ginger cooky man, and you put currants for eyes, nose, and mouth and for coat buttons down the front. Children had a lot of fun helping when cookies were being made, lapping the bowl when all was done! The modern cooky cutters continue to be made in various shapes, but a collector of tinware detects the difference between the early tin and the modern tin by the way the cutter is made.

The doughnut cutter made of wood or tin dates back several generations. Not always were the center balls fried as ball doughnuts, but more often they were mixed with the rest of the dough and used as doughnuts, until the last cutting left a few which went into the kettle. How we children did love those extra balls! The old iron kettles for deep-fat frying are still holding forth in many homes, for there seems to be nothing better in the modern market. Records show that doughnuts have been found in almost every country and at a very early date. The recipe for doughnuts may have come to this country with the first immigrants, but it was in 1673 that a Mrs. Anna Joralemon opened the first doughnut-shop in New York. A plaque to commemo-

PLATE 98. *This maple-sugar skimmer was made with a semicircular edge to fit the contour of the kettles.*

rate the invention of the hole was erected to Captain Hanson Crockett Gregory of Camden, Maine, November 2, 1947, one hundred years after he was said to have come across the idea of a doughnut with a hole.*

Tin scoops, spatulas, strainers, and skimmers were among the listed tinware. The skimmers were handleless or had long handles of tin or of wood. Tin strainers were made following the old horse-hair sieves, with a rim and bottom, the bottom perforated with holes. There were small strainers and large strainers. Many early ones were made with a wire-mesh head and with handles to scoop or skim. If the bottom was made of tin and had large holes, the piece was called a colander and often was made part of a steamer, the colander fitting over a pot which held water. In early days, the only method of cooking was roasting or boiling in a pot, but as time progressed, the science of cooking also advanced and many methods were discovered to vary the cooking of food. No kitchen was complete without a steamer, which was used principally for fish.

* Mrs. Josephine H. Pierce

Tin scoops were very necessary and are still seen in every pantry, half cylindrical with a sturdy handle at the end, some broad and short, some long and slender. Our family scoops are still being used in a tin holder of sugar and a tin holder of flour.

A handy flour sifter was made with a combination of scoop and sifter. Meals were kept in barrels; rye, Indian or "injun," wheat, and oatmeal. The gristmills, with their huge stones turned by water power, ground the kernels that were brought to the mill by the owners, grown and harvested by many families. The miller was a jolly fellow, and much has been written in prose and poetry about the "dusty miller." Perhaps to him there was music in the whirr of the big paddle wheel, the fall of the water, and the ring of the machinery as the stones ground out a certain amount of meal in pay for the grinding, to sell to those who had

PLATE 99. *Tin scoops of the type shown here have endured the ages and are still commonly found in use. The tray in the front is a muffin pan of rather crude workmanship. To the right and left are, respectively, a flour shaker and a schoolroom dipper for water.*

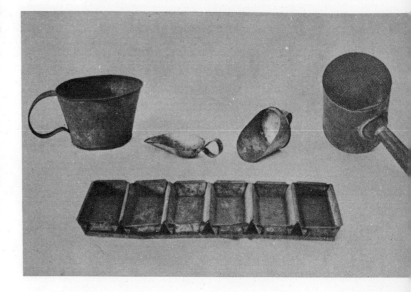

PLATE 100. *Ingenious combination sifter-scoops were made for greater convenience and efficiency in the kitchen. Both scoops on this page were patented in 1866.*

no grain. By another generation and yet another, every family was buying flour by the barrel, as they bought sugar by the barrel, from the country store. Today, one may see real country stores and see old gristmills come to life again. Stone-ground meal can be had and with it goes the full flavor of the meal that contains all the nutritive value plus the romance that went into its grinding.

The scoop sifter is an ingenious thing and would not be out of place in today's pantry or cupboard, even though the modern hurried and harried generations buy flour in small quantities, sometimes even in a three-pound bag. The two sides of the sifter are curved at the back to fit the shape of the sifter, which is covered with a fine wire mesh. A sturdy handle extends from the back of the scoop. Inside the scoop, placed against the wire mesh, is a wheel which has two circular ends with five wires running between. A crank on the outside turned the wheel which pushed out the flour. The mouth of the sifter is straight and wide. It seems such a practical idea to scoop up

a large amount of flour from the barrel, hold it over a tin or crockery pan, and grind the crank. The scoop sifter shown here measures about eight inches across and ten inches in length. It has a label on the top, nearly all of which is still legible. It was made by P. Bucknam, Portland, Maine. It was called the Bucknam Improved Combination Sifter and was patented on May 13, 1866, "State and County Rights for sale by the Proprietor."

Another sifter in the museum seems to have been one step ahead of the larger one. The wheel inside has four tin paddles that would push out the sifted flour more thoroughly than the five rods of the other sifter. The handle of this smaller one is on top, which again would make the job of holding the sifter while scooping and sifting much easier. This one has a patent stamped in the tip of the scoop, "Earnshaw's Patent, July 25, 1866." It would be interesting to search the records and find out who made such tinware and where the factories were located. Little has been recorded.

Wooden lemon squeezers with two hinged

PLATE 101. *This combination sifter-scoop had paddles rotating inside to sift the flour.*

PLATES 102 & 103. *The two pudding molds on the left have copper bases, which allowed for a sharper design. To the right is an early mold fashioned from a single sheet of tin. It is owned by the Brigham family of Worcester, Massachusetts.*

arms are not more than seventy-five or eighty years old. The museum boasts of many that are unusual. On the inside of one arm is a half dome, and on the other arm is a round hollow with holes, to fit the dome. The half lemon was placed over the holes, pulp-side up. When the two arms were squeezed together, the dome projection squeezed out the juice. The rind was then inside out. Two squeezers were made on stands so a tumbler could be placed underneath to catch the juices. One of these is different from the others and is patented because it has two heavy blades at the end, which worked with the arms. These cut the lemon before it was put between the arms and squeezed.

A plain wooden squeezer was used in our family. Then one was found with an ironstone head and cup, another one with a lignum-vitae head and cup, and a third one with a tin head and cup. A large squeezer was used at picnics, held over a wooden tub, and in this squeezer the juice ran out of holes at the side of the cup, so the squeezer could be rested on the tub when it was used. It measures nearly two feet long. These are a far cry from the modern electric squeezers

or juicers run by electricity and operated by a button.

Among the most artistic of the array of tin pantry tools are the pudding molds. Puddings came when more time could be given to making attractive desserts, and molds are found in pottery and tin. Those of tin were made with fluted sides, a bottom with a design and a narrow skirt on which the mold stood. Copper was used for the bottom, for copper could take a sharper design. Then the copper was tinned over together with the rest of the mold. The mold at the left in the illustration shows the copper base where the tin has worn off. The designs were most varied, copying those that were used on butter molds and prints, such as wheat or other grains, flowers, and fruit. An early mold has no skirt, and the bottom is flat, allowing the mold to stand up. This appears to be older than the molds that had a skirt. These pudding molds are commonly used today for puddings and jellies. The pottery ones make attractive holders for flowers. Tin molds have a tendency to rust and hence more care has to be given to them.

PLATE 104. *A tin cooking utensil with a cover, for the stove top.*

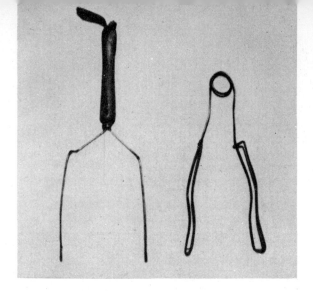

PLATE 106. *Tools for lifting bread loaves, pies, and puddings were numerous in number as well as in style. Both pie lifters shown here are made of wire.*

Cooking utensils for the stove top were common and many were artistic in shape. One illustrated is oval and has a handle and a cover with a ring. Some of the tin utensils were used as tableware, such as one that had a hot-water holder and on this was a serving dish with cover. Food could be served and kept warm in such an arrangement. Most of these have a fancy britannia handle.

When baking was done in the days of the brick ovens, bread and pies and puddings were put into the oven with long-handled peels or shovels. When the cookstove came into existence, there was little need for long handles. To lift out the bread, pies, and puddings there were many varieties of tools. One was shaped like a small pitchfork, another one has two arms of wire at the end of a coil spring. Shown here is a tin pie lifter made like a round shovel with a

short wooden handle which may have been used for other things besides pies. These hung near the stove.

Muffin pans, cake pans, and bread pans were made of tin and they must have been a relief from the heavy iron utensils of previous generations. Tin cups and tin dippers were necessary articles. A long-handled tin dipper is always associated with the one-room schoolhouse and seemed as much a part of it as were the slates, the big brass bell, the stove, and the wood pile.

Coffeepots and teapots were among the first of the tinware to be made. Coffee drinking was quite common by the time of the Revolution, and tea was fully as popular. At first the coffee bean was boiled whole, which of course made a very tasteless drink. Then came the roasters that roasted the beans which were then ground before using. Neither was tea appreciated when it was first introduced. The leaves were boiled, the water poured off, and butter and salt were added to the boiled leaves, which must have been eaten with little relish. In due

PLATE 105. *This pie peel was made like a flat, round shovel and was used for taking pies and pots from the oven.*

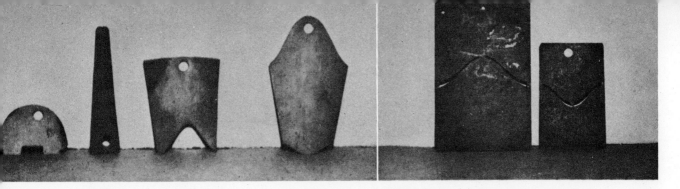

PLATES 107 & 108. *The more complex tin utensils were often made with as many as fourteen sections welded together. To cut these sections accurately, templets like those shown here were used by the tinsmith. From the Bailey collection.*

time, tea leaves were boiled and the liquid was used as a drink.

The earliest tin utensils, as has been stated, were made in sections, cut with templets or patterns. At times as many as fourteen pieces went into the making of a single pot. The pieces were either seamed together or soldered together. The lines of the early pots were most artistic. A coffeepot owned by Mrs. Bailey was made of pricked tin, the early way of making a design, before painting or stencilling was originated. Pricking was done with a sharp tool, the sections placed on a board for the operation. A design was first planned and great care was taken not to pierce the tin entirely through. The sections were pierced from the inside, leaving the rough points outside. After the receptacle was finished and the sections seamed together, the inside was washed with a thin coat of tin which sealed the holes and made the pot or pitcher watertight.

A very lovely teapot owned by the late Frank K. Swain shows an exquisite design also done by pricking. The spout and the top of the pot are ribbed, which is a process done with a blunt tool. The design is on the base of the pot and on the body, showing remarkable workmanship.

The difference between a teapot and a coffeepot seems to be in the spout, the teapot having a curved spout of one piece and the coffeepot having a long, jointed spout.

One of the teapots shown here has a ribbed design on the spout and on the body. This is as graceful and beautiful as any pot of fine china. Pictured with the ribbed teapot is a beautiful pitcher, which has some of the sections ribbed and a pricked design on the neck. Both types of work were done with special tools and a hammer. These pieces were loaned by Mrs. Bailey for me to photograph. Still another piece is the large

PLATE 109. *The delicate design on this beautiful teapot from the collection of the late Frank K. Swain of Doylestown, Pennsylvania, was done by pricking the sections before they were welded together into shape.*

❧ 61 ❧ *Household Utensils of Tin*

PLATE 110. *These are two beautiful examples showing the excellent workmanship of the early tinsmiths. Ribbed designs like the designs on these two pieces were commonly used on tinware. From the collection of Mrs. G.W.B. Bailey.*

PLATE 111. *Also from the Bailey collection is this nine-quart tin pitcher with a set of tin tumblers.*

PLATE 112. *A double-sectioned pot used for chocolate. The outer section, which has a mouth above the handle, held hot water to keep the chocolate warm. The handle and knob are made of britannia.*

nine-quart measure or jug with four tall tumblers of tin. Pricked and ribbed work was peculiar to Pennsylvania.

Two coffeepots are illustrated, the smaller one with a painted design accredited to Pennsylvania. The large pot looks like an all-service pot, holding a gallon. The families were large, and the guests in any tavern were many, so such a large coffeepot was quite necessary. The handle is on the side, which is somewhat unusual, and on the lower part of the back is another small handle by which the pot was lifted as the coffee was being poured. This pot seems typical of early New England.

The various tinsmiths created their own versions of pots and there is a great variety of them. A coffeepot was called a coffee filter if it was made in sections, one resting upon the other. One, illustrated, has three sections. The upper part has a piece of fine

PLATE 113. *The spout of the coffeepot was made in sections like the one shown on the right, whereas that of the teapot was molded out of a single piece like the one on the left. These two pots, accredited to the Pennsylvania Dutch, are also from the Bailey collection.*

homespun linen fastened over the bottom, and the liquid from the boiling water and the coffee grounds filtered down to the center section. That, too, has a piece of linen fastened over it, so by the time the liquid reached the bottom container, it was clear and ready to be poured into cups. This arrangement was a forerunner of the percolator of today.

There is a teapot with two sections, an inner one and an outer one. The inner one was for tea and the outer one was for hot water, used if necessary to weaken the tea. The spout for the tea is in the front and that for the water is on one side. Such a container was made for the convenience it afforded.

A double pot with only one spout was made for chocolate, which appeared as a drink first in 1697, the bean coming from South America and the West Indies. The inside section of the pot was for chocolate,

PLATE 116. *This teapot from the Society for the Preservation of New England Antiquities has outer and inner sections with separate spouts. The inner section with the spout on the front was used for tea, and the outer section with the spout on the side was used for hot water.*

and the outer for hot water. Above the handle is an outlet into which the water was poured and out of which the steam escaped. This hot water kept the chocolate hot for a longer time. The pot was made of tin and britannia. The handle, spout, lip, and tip of the cover are britannia, making a more decorative pot than if it had been made entirely of tin. Britannia was used for decoration on tin.

PLATES 114 & 115. *A prototype of the modern percolator, this coffeepot had two sections with cloth filters to filter the coffee. The small cup standing by the pot was used for measuring the coffee. From the collection of the Society for the Preservation of New England Antiquities.*

PLATES 117 & 118. *This pail, used to carry animal feed in the farms, also has double sections. The outer section connected with the large spout held hot water to keep the mash warm. A vent connected with the inner section protrudes into the spout to allow the steam to escape when the lid was closed.*

Carrying out the same principle of double sections is the large pail. The pail at first glance looks like an ordinary pail. But there are two floors, one within the other. A large spout connects with the outer part into which hot water was poured, and inside that spout is a smaller one connected with the inner section to let the steam escape when the lid was put on. The pail was used for animal feed, such as mash for young calves, and the hot water kept the mash hot until the barn was reached and the animals fed. The cover is double sealed, which held the heat better than a single cover. In the early days, mash was made in the big brass

PLATE 119. *This large all-service pot held a gallon and had two handles for easier handling.*

or copper kettle in the set-kettle fireplace, the brick fireplace that was connected with a chimney in the ell of the house and which had a fire under it. That same kettle was used when boiling clothes on washday and, after it had been scoured with vinegar and salt, it was used when making apple butter in the fall of the year.

From the museum in Doylestown, Pennsylvania came a picture of a tin nursing can. The two views of it show the operation of the spout, which extends down inside the can, within one-eighth of an inch from the bottom. The can is four inches high and two and one-half inches in diameter at the bottom and one and five-eighths inches at the top. This single nursing can was owned by the late Mr. Swain, and the museum has a can for twins, with two spouts, at right angles to each other. These cans are rare, for only in extreme cases was a baby "bottle fed." Such a can is owned by James A. Keillor of Wading River, Long Island, and still another is found in the Hingham Historical Society, Hingham, Massachusetts.

A novelty in the way of a lunch box shows

ingenuity. There are four sections and a
cover, each section fitting upon the other,
tapering in size toward the bottom. A long
wire handle, fastened to the bottom section,
clamps up over the entire box when closed.
Three sections were for food; the fourth,
the bottom, has a deep, fitted round cover,
which when taken out and inverted made
a cup. This shows that the bottom section
held a drink of some sort, completing a meal
that could include everything necessary. It
would seem that this was a school lunch box.
Sandwiches, pie, doughnuts, and a chunk
of cheese, together with the drink of milk
and a tin cup—what more could a school
child ask for!

An interesting tool was the tin hatchel.
A piece of wood was entirely covered with
tin, folded over at the ends. Then the long
nails were driven through the tin and the
board. It is a work of art and would outlast
any hatchel made on a wooden plank. The
hatchel was used in the process of freeing
the flax from poor fibres, the flax being
drawn through the long teeth. The story of

PLATES 122 & 123.
*This rare nursing can
comes from the collec-
tion of the late Frank
K. Swain. There is
also another model
with two spouts for
feeding twins.*

PLATES 120 & 121. *A full meal could be stored in
this ingenious lunch box. The bottom section was used
for keeping a drink of some sort and had a lid, which
when inverted could be used as a cup.*

Household Utensils of Tin

PLATE 124. *Hatchels like this were used to free the flax from poor fibres before it was used for making linen thread. The baseboard on this one is covered with sheet tin. From the collection of Isabel Gordon.*

flax, from the growing of it to the linen threads, woven on looms, is fully described in *Home Life in Colonial Days* by Alice Morse Earle and in my book *The Early American House.*

Specimen boxes were not too unlike the tin candlebox. The candlebox has two narrow arms that extend at the back with rings at the end so the box could be hung on the wall. After the candles had been made, they were stored in a pine candlebox with a sliding cover and kept from the light, for light turned the candles yellow. A housewife's pride was in her white candles. A few days' supply was kept in the tin candlebox ready for use.

The specimen boxes were used by botanists or other naturalists to hold the results of a day's excursion. These boxes have rings at the ends of the top through which a strap could be strung and slung over the shoulder. One of the boxes illustrated has a cover the length of the box which lifts up by a hasp, and the other has a shorter cover that opens from the top down. This box has a handle on the top by which the box could be carried

even though there was a strap that slung over the shoulder.

There is a possibility that these boxes were used by a tinker for his tools, for the boxes are early and tinkers came before naturalists. They are long enough and large enough to have been used for tools, one measuring two feet long. There is no definite proof. The dealer might have sensed this possibility, for the price of the long box was eight dollars.

If anyone has not seen an old country store, either reproduced or one that has survived the years, he has missed a thrill. There are many today, in small towns and

PLATES 125 & 126. *Specimen boxes for naturalists were made much like the tinker's pig and may have also been used as such by the tinker for his tools.*

PLATE 127. *In the old country stores there would invariably be a hanging scale suspended over the counter.*

also maintained completely reproduced in museums. It is the odor that greets one first; the odor of coffee, spices, apples, together with a mustiness and the faint smell of burning wood from the wood-burning stove. Counters line the walls, and the post-office boxes are at one end. The cracker barrel occupies a conspicuous place out front, a barrel of apples stands beside it, and the pot-bellied stove with a rail, where the feet rested, is in the middle of the room, radiating heat for the entire store. A box filled with sawdust surrounds the stove, and a gay-looking Bennington spittoon stands by. Two bar chairs are drawn up to the friendliness of the stove, and between them is a checkerboard resting on a keg of nails, with the black and red men set for a game. Overhead are hanging buckets, sieves, dried herbs, baskets, and other things for sale. Behind a counter stands a cabinet of small drawers, each one labelled with the name of the contents. Quite likely, the cabinet is

painted wagon-wheel blue. Old school-slates stand in various places, announcing some of the important purchases, such as BUTTER 25¢ A PD., MILK 5¢ A QT., EGGS 25¢ A DOZ.

The candy counter never misses in its supply of penny candy, displayed in glass dishes; old fashioned chocolate drops, colored bananas, long licorice whips, striped peppermint sticks, candy cigarettes, chocolate and licorice pipes, little tin dishes filled with soft candy with a spoon added, gum drops—nothing is skipped. Two for a cent, a penny apiece, and what a lot for a nickle! And the candy you buy is put into a striped paper bag!

A red scale is on the counter, with weights and a boat-shaped tray of brass in which purchases could be weighed, such as meal, flour, sugar, or crackers. Tin scoops, big and little, are near at hand, ready to be used. Hanging over one of the counters is a scale with a center fulcrum and two arms.

PLATE 128. *A steelyard was also frequently used. This sturdy tin pan was used on the end of the steelyard for holding the merchandise to be weighed.*

PLATE 129. *Many types of apple driers were devised over the years. This one, patented in 1886, used steam, passing through the double tin shelves, to dry the slices.*

One arm holds a big tin scoop swung on three chains, and the other arm holds a tin dish, although some of the scales have a wooden plate. The scoop held the article to be weighed, and the plate held the weights. This type of scale is older than the red scale on a standard. Another scale for weighing is the steelyard, a fulcrum and one arm that carried the pear-shaped weight, which was moved along in graded notches. This hangs from the ceiling. Under the fulcrum, a pan is suspended by long arms. Some pans are of tin, some of copper, measuring as much as a foot in diameter. These steelyards range from small sizes to those that could weigh three hundred pounds.

Dried apples were commonly found in all country stores. They were sold until well toward the end of the nineteenth century and used to tide over the months when there

were no apples and when apple pies were a necessary part of the meal. There were two ways of drying apples. One way was to pare and core them and then quarter them. The quarters were strung on a heavy, yard-long thread with a big needle. The strings were dried and then packed away in boxes. The other method was to pare and core the apples and then slice them. This made apple rings. There were wooden parers and iron parers and inventions that cored as well as pared.

Apple driers were a necessary part of the home, for every family dried and stored their apples. Most of the driers were made of splint. A drying house was one of the various houses of a Shaker settlement, where there was a heating apparatus and places to set the apple quarters or slices. There is an old Shaker drying house of brick in the once-thriving colony of Shakers at Harvard, Massachusetts. The Shakers made their dried apples only for their own consumption, but other colonists sold or bartered theirs at a country store, besides supplying their own tables.

Coming to the years of patented productions, a tin apple drier has been found that dried by steam. The patent reads:

BURNER & ANDERSON
Common Sense
Fruit
Evaporator
Pat'd April 20 1886
NEWARK O.

It measures twenty-six inches long, twenty-two inches wide, and eighteen inches high. Three floors set on uprights, all of tin, each floor is a sealed container, two being one inch in depth and one three inches deep, all with a narrow rim around the edge. The upper floor slants slightly, the middle floor slants in the opposite direction, and the lower floor is level. Tubes connect the three floors. Hot water was poured into an opening with a screw top in the bottom floor, while the evaporator rested on a stove top or some other heating arrangement. The heated water created steam which rose through the tubes up to each floor and out a small chimney-like vent at the top. The apple slices were placed on each floor and were not disturbed while the process was going on. There are no directions to say how long the slices remained on the shelves, but any housewife could tell when they were ready to be taken off. After they had cooled, they were stored away in boxes or other containers.

It became a regular habit to dry apples, and if none were to be had from the family's orchard, the country store could supply the demand. When a pie was to be made, soaking the apples in water produced juicy, natural slices, and dried apple pies seemed to satisfy the family during the long winter months. Scientific research gives us the exact moisture content of the slices of apples prepared in the various ways; the following data was obtained from the Extension Food Technology Department, University of Massachusetts. Evaporated apples have a moisture content of approximately twenty-five per cent, dried apples contain about twelve per cent, and dehydrated apples about three-fifths of one per cent moisture. It would show then that the early method of drying apples was superior to that of evaporating the slices.

Many things found today bring up a discussion as to why certain pieces were made

and how they were used in the early days. Most tools and utensils could fill more than one use, but a collector likes to reason out why the piece was originally made. A sifter of tin with a long handle came up for discussion. The head is like a colander with slanting sides, a foot in diameter with holes half an inch in diameter in the bottom. A short tubular handle is riveted to the head and held firmly by two braces. A yard-long wooden handle was set into the tin handle. This was a sifter of some kind and the long handle showed it was used near heat, the user standing back from the source of heat. The solution reached is that it was used in a charcoal kiln.

Many families made their own charcoal from the wood on their land, preferably maple or birch; white poplar and willow was also sometimes used. Often there was one man in the village who made and sold charcoal to the community. The common way to set up a kiln was to dig a circular trench and stand the peeled logs end up, two or three deep, coming to a point like a tepee. The logs were then covered with sod. Holes were left at the bottom for the air to get in, and an open space was left at

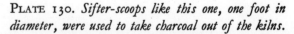

PLATE 130. *Sifter-scoops like this one, one foot in diameter, were used to take charcoal out of the kilns.*

the top to serve as a flue. The pile was set on fire by putting burning wood into the top opening. The fire gradually burned from the top to the bottom and from the center to the outside of the pile. As the center burned away, fresh wood was thrown in at the top, so as to keep the heap quite full. The smoke was thick and white when the work was going on properly; if it became thin with a blue flame, the wood was burning too fast. The combustion was then checked by closing the holes at the bottom. As soon as the combustion was completed, the pile was entirely covered with sod and left to cool for two or three days. It was then taken to pieces, and if the wood, then turned to charcoal, was still hot, sand was thrown onto it to cool it. It has. been found that one hundred parts of wood yielded sixty-one to sixty-five parts of charcoal. To lift the charcoal from the pit, such a sifter as the long-handled sifter of tin was used. But more often a splint charcoal sifter was used, taking a larger amount in one scoopful. The powder fell through the holes, and the pieces of charcoal were put into barrels or tubs.

Charcoal was used as fuel, making a very hot heat, in tin biscuit ovens with pots, in braziers, or iron holders for burning coals, in foot stoves, and later in flatirons that burned charcoal for heat when ironing, a product of the late nineteenth century. Charcoal powder was used in medicine powders and in fertilizers for gardens. There were no books on chemistry in the old days, but the colonists learned much from the Indians and from experience, which often proved to be as valuable as lessons learned from books.

PLATE 131. *This primitive shower bath, owned by Elmer Keith of Clintonville, Connecticut, was patented in 1845 and has a water holder, one foot in diameter.*

The history of baths and bathing is little known, but is extremely interesting. It stems from Greek mythology into the time of the Phoenicians, Greeks, and Romans. And, passing down the years, a few relics remain for a collector to acquire.

When I began collecting woodenware in 1932, I had a ninety-year-old friend with whom I occasionally visited, Annie Chandler Worth. She had come from down East and her early life on the farm had been filled with facts worth recording. Much of this life she told to me. She began school at three years of age at the District Country

School; she took notes for her father at the time of his invention of a plow, when she was thirteen; at fifteen, she took charge of the post office in one room of the home, folding and stamping the letters. When she was left a widow with three children, she taught school and carried on her home.

When Annie was five years old, her father was subject to headaches. The family had seen an advertisement of a patent shower bath sold in Boston and straightaway sent an order for the affair. When it arrived, it was rigged up in the attic. According to my friend's description, there was a frame around which hung a curtain. On the top were rods running across, and onto this was placed the holder that held the water. A long cord was tied to a ring in the handle of the holder. The patient stood in a tub within the curtain, and when he pulled the cord, the water was released.

Mother and the little girl were there in the attic, when father, stripped of his clothes, stepped into the tub within the curtain. When the water, which the directions said should be cold, was released and showered upon the patient, the shocked father dashed out of the curtain, down the narrow attic stairs, and into his bedroom. Mother and the little girl were too stunned to move, the curses that came from below made matters worse. The patent shower was never tried again, headache or no headache.

Seventeen years after I was told the story of that shower bath, I was in a library looking over old issues of the magazine *Antique*. Toward the end of an issue of 1935, I found a picture of the container for the water of an early shower bath. Written on it was, "Waterman, patented August 1,

1869." This container was found down Maine. I immediately tied it up with the story of my ninety-year-old friend, made a sketch of it in my notebook, and recorded the name and date, to use in my book on tinware.

One year after finding the account of the shower-bath can, I went to see a dealer friend who is particularly interested in the more unusual pieces. She greeted me with much excitement in her face for she had found a curious thing of tin. When she showed it to me, I said, "the shower-bath can!" I could not believe my eyes. It is a sealed can, painted cream color, with perforations in the bottom and a spring at the top, controlled by a lever. This lever

PLATE 132. *This two-quart water can for a shower bath has a perforated bottom. The water was released by pulling on a cord attached to the wire extending down the side of the can. Patented in 1869.*

PLATES 133 & 134. *Foot tubs like these were among the common household utensils of tin. The one on the right was called a "hat tub." The patient sat on the built-in platform on the right. The hat tub is from the collection of Stanley Atherton of Bolton, Massachusetts.*

has a wire attached to it which has a ring at the end where a long cord was tied, reaching down into the enclosed frame. The can held two quarts of water. My friend and I went to the kitchen sink and set the can in a basin of water. By releasing the spring and holding it, the water was sucked in, filling the can. Then when the spring was released again, the water sprayed out from the holes, like a watering pot. Finding this shower-bath can came as a climax to the story of the shower bath set up in the attic more than eighty years previously. A collector's life is never without exciting moments.

Many were the sitz tubs and foot tubs. The sitz tub in my family was painted green with a white lining. It was like an armchair resting on the floor with no legs, a high back, and arms. The patient sat in the tub with legs and feet extending out to the floor,

a blanket over them. Sitting in the warm bath, the patient would be able to relax and seek relief from many ailments, such as colds, chills, or cramps. The family gave away the green sitz tub in the drive for metals in the Second World War. So my museum lost a good piece from the collection of tin.

Foot tubs were small. The patient sat in a chair, with his feet in the tub. The small tub illustrated has a place for the soap at one side. The tub is about thirty inches long and is painted brown with a white lining. Still another tub was the "hat tub." This is shaped like a huge brimmed hat, the width of the span of a man's arms. The patient sat on a seat built on one side of the brim with his feet in the center basin, the crown of the hat. At one side is a holder for the soap and under the seat is an outlet through which the water could be emptied.

Antique Tin & Tole Ware ❧ 72 ❧

Many such tubs took the place of bathtubs.

The huge wooden tub in the illustration measures nearly three feet across. Such a tub was dragged in from the woodshed and placed in front of the huge fireplace on Saturday nights. It was the family tub and it held sway for more than one generation. This tub was borrowed from my museum to appear in the play *A Cotter's Saturday Night*.

Bathtubs did not appear until the nineteenth century. The first tubs were made of wood and lined with tin, and a cock in the bottom allowed the water to be drawn off. These tubs stood on casters and could be wheeled about. Dr. Cecil Drinker, former Dean of the Harvard School of Public Health, stated that the diary of his grandmother told of the first bathtub to appear in Philadelphia in 1803. The diary reads: "My husband went into ye tepid bath before dinner. He hensel'd (tried out) a new bathing tub bought yesterday for $17 made of wood and lined with thin (tin) and painted, with castors under ye bottom and a brass cock to let out the water."

In Waltham is a brick mansion which was built during 1803–1804 by Governor Christopher Gore. Gore was a Revolutionary soldier, a statesman, and later Governor of Massachusetts. In a small lower room of the mansion was a bathtub, said to have been of lead, standing on casters. In the ceiling overhead is a hole which can be seen today, although the bathtub is no longer there. A short pipe extended from the hole, and when the Governor wished to have a bath, a servant went overhead and poured water on his master as he sat in the tub. This was another form of a shower bath, which seemed to have been the first method conceived for ablutions, after the days of the open fire and of the Saturday night tub-standings on the hearth.

Tracing back the history of the Turkish bath, the research worker finds it accredited to the Romans. The ruins of the Phoenicians, the Greeks, and the Romans show that baths were an important part of their daily life. Cinders and other signs of existence of baths have been found in excavations. It has been recorded that Athena instructed Hercules how to use certain baths, so as to recover his strength after severe exertions, and that Andromache prepared a hot bath for her husband Hector on his return from battle.

The Romans acquired the bath after they had conquered the Greeks, and it then rose to a pitch of splendor and luxury. In those ancient days in Rome, there were rooms where the body was "lubricated" with oil and a gymnasium where various exercises and games were practiced following the bath. This Roman bath changed to the Turkish bath, and the bather entered a room of high temperature, where he reclined. This temperature caused perspiration. Then he passed into another room with still higher

PLATE 135. *Huge tubs like the one shown here were used in front of the fireplace for the family Saturday-night bath.*

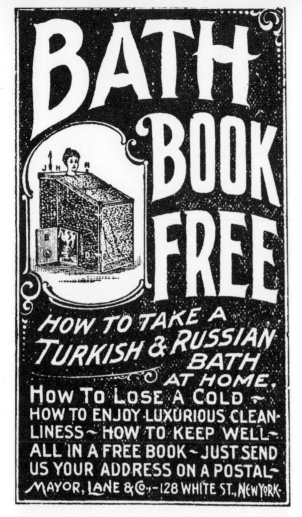

PLATE 136. *In the Gay Nineties a fad for Turkish baths developed. This advertisement appeared in the magazine the* Delineator *in 1890.*

temperature. After this he went through a process of cooling down and finally he rested for half an hour, sipped coffee, and then dressed for the outer world again.

The generally known "Turkish bath" taken at home was accomplished with a lamp placed under a chair, the bather enveloped in blankets, which caused perspiration to break out. The body was then bathed in tepid water, and the bather rested until the skin felt cool and comfortable. It was in the Gay Nineties that the Turkish bath appeared again. The illustrated advertisement appeared in a magazine in 1890 and it shows the cabinet in use. It was a frame covered with a rubberized

cloth, with a door in the front through which the patient entered to sit on a stool inside, and an opening in the top through which the patient thrust his head. The heat for the bath, or rather for the steaming, was provided by a tin lamp burning kerosene oil. This outfit for curing colds and for making better health was very popular over a period of years, and many were the home-made cabinets set up by amateurs. Establishments that gave Turkish baths were located in business sections of cities and it proved not only a popular fad but a profitable business.

A steam bath was another way of cleaning the body and invigorating the blood. This method is practiced in this country among many people who still retain the customs of the old country, especially the Finns. In the steam house or cabin is a large brick oven with an opening with a door near the floor. A chimney extends out through a hole in the wall. The top of the oven is covered with small stones. A tub partly filled with water

PLATE 137. *Steam baths were patterned after those used in Europe, especially Finland. Water was poured over the stones on the furnace to generate steam.*

rests on the stones. When the stones are heated, water is poured onto them, generating steam, which fills the cabin. The bather sits on a bench or reclines if he chooses to and rests. A bundle of small birch twigs had been made into a switch and with this, the bather switches himself to stimulate the blood. He continues to pour water over the stones until there is sufficient steam in the cabin. Drying himself with a towel, he steps into the anteroom and dresses.

An advertisement for a tin dishwasher shows what could have been the forerunner of today's electric washer. An open section shows the arrangement of the dishes inside the holder. A crank at the top revolved the rack holding the dishes and, according to the advertisement, "it washes, rinces *(sic)*, dries and polishes the dishes at once." This

PLATE 138. *With the progress of time, such "humane devices" as this dishwasher appeared on the market to alleviate the tasks of the house wife. This advertisement is also from an issue of the* Delineator *in 1890.*

PLATE 139. *Tin pitchers were used to carry hot water to the chambers in taverns. The one on the left with a cover and a wood-grain pattern is of a more recent period than the other, painted pumpkin yellow.*

must have been one of the first mechanical dishwashers.

A rare find was the tall tin pitcher, painted pumpkin yellow. It stands eighteen inches high, including the uplifted snout, and the base has a diameter of ten inches. There is also a second pitcher which is painted wagon-wheel blue, the same color that was commonly used to paint the spokes of the farm wagons. These two colors, the pumpkin yellow and the blue, were popular colors in the long ago, together with the Indian red. The red and yellow clay in the soil was the base for pumpkin yellow, mixed with whites of eggs or skim milk and later with neat's-foot oil, the substance obtained from the hoofs of oxen called neat cattle. The color blue of the early days was obtained from the indigo plant, first imported and later

Household Utensils of Tin

PLATE 140. *In the ballrooms of the taverns, fiddlers used to play on fiddler's seats such as this one found in a tavern in New Hampshire. From the Society for the Preservation of New England Antiquities.*

cultivated in various localities for use as a dye.*

The yellow tin pitcher is an early piece as told by the workmanship and by the type of design. With tin, it is not only the quality of the tin plate and the way the seams are put together that are useful in determining the age of a piece, but also the apparent purpose for which the piece was made. The story of the yellow pitcher is that it was once used in a tavern to carry warm water to the guests in the morning, from room to room. Visualizing the use of the yellow pitcher gives one an incentive to know more about taverns and the life in them.

When I first became interested in collect-

* Gould, *The Early American House.*

ing wooden pantry boxes, no antique sign escaped my notice. A sign on an old tavern caught my eye one day while in Vermont, and I stopped to see the antiques on display. This happened in 1935, and although my recollection of the antiques has completely faded, no progress of the years can ever take away the memory of the old tavern.

Entering the front door—there was a door on each of the three sides of the tavern—we stepped into a long hallway. On the left was the barroom, with a bar in one corner over which dropped a portcullis or grating. A huge fireplace with a wide, stone hearth took up nearly one side of the room. To be told that Daniel Webster had often stopped there on his way home to Salisbury,

PLATE 141. *Pitchers for the chamber were gaily decorated in color. This pitcher is painted green with a decoration of autumn leaves. From the collection of Mrs. Harry Mirick of Princeton, Massachusetts.*

Antique Tin & Tole Ware ⚜ 76 ⚜

Vermont, had little significance to us, even though he had sat in that barroom, had danced in the ballroom, and the bed in which he had slept was still to be seen.

At the front of the house on the second floor was a ballroom with its dome ceiling and narrow box seats around the room with lids that lifted and into which outer garments were placed. The fiddler's seat was at one side, a small round platform with a rail and a small round seat, so the fiddler might sit or stand as he scraped away on his fiddle and called the dances, the Quadrille, the Portland Fancy, and other square dances.

We were asked if we would like to go to the third floor, and there at the head of the narrow steep stairs were three small rooms, alloted to stagecoach drivers. In each room was one window and in the corner a low bunk. At the front side of the bunk, two or three strips of sheathing had been left out, and into this opening, the stagecoach driver thrust his boots. Wrapped in quilts and lying on straw, the driver slept his alloted time, ready to continue on his journey or to return with the coach that met him coming from the other way. Stagecoach drivers drove an alloted distance of not more than thirty miles, and either four or six horses were on the coach. That stone tavern built in the late eighteenth century was something not easily forgotten.

It must have been a joy to fit up the chambers of the homes with tinware, instead of using the best crockery sets. The best sets graced the guest room at all times, standing on the commode or the washstand. There were many pieces in a set—my family still has a complete set. It consists of a bowl and pitcher, covered soap dish, toothbrush

PLATE 142. *This pitcher is painted a beautiful cream color and is from the collection of Mrs. Theresa Richardson of Princeton, Massachusetts.*

holder, small pitcher for hot water, slop pail with a cover, and a covered chamber pot or, in the vernacular, a vessel. Some sets are very beautiful, with colored bands and decorations. The water pitcher is often most artistically shaped.

When tin usurped the place of breakable china, the chamber set of china was kept in the guest room. In the other bedrooms, the china bowl remained, but the pitcher or waterpot was of tin. These were gaily decorated in color, the one illustrated being a delicate green with sprays of autumn leaves in natural colors. The waterpot stands twenty inches high. The lines are artistic as are those of another pitcher, painted cream with no decoration. These stood on the floor, never in the bowl.

When I was a little girl, our family vacationed in nearby Paxton in an old house, once a bootshop, made into a fine home. It

PLATE 143. *Slop pails were part of the chamber set. This one painted mottled brown is from the collection of Mrs. Mary Johnson of Barre, Massachusetts.*

was owned by my uncle and aunt. The house held many attractions for me, and I used to love to go to bed carrying an old tin candle-holder, shielding the feeble flame of the candle with my hand so it would not go out and leave me in the dark as I went upstairs to bed. How well I remember the tin water-pot and the tin slop pail! Collectors' items today! The slop pail was painted brown with a blue lining and it had a corrugated cover that set inside, sloping toward the center like a fan. In the middle of the cover was a hole over which was a raised round projection. This served as a handle by which to take off the cover. I remember watching the water run down the slanting sides into the hole and down into the pail.

A strange find not too long ago was a holder for the chamber pot. It looks much like a cakebox of tin, painted gray with a decoration of flowers on the sides. This stood on the floor by the washstand, a gay note of color added to the color of the other tinware.

There were tin soap dishes, tin shaving cups with brush and soap, small tin pitchers, and various tin holders. There were tin washbasins, but the crockery bowl seemed to hold sway even when the accompanying pieces were tin. Even a tin bedpan came to light. It has a cover for the opening and a small cover for the outlet, fastened together with a chain. It is heavy and not unlike pewter in appearance. It was another house-hold necessity at the time when tin reigned.

My uncle who owned the old red house in the country was a minister. He went to Europe more than once, and on one of the trips when he went with John B. Gough, the great temperance leader, he brought

PLATE 144. *An elaborately decorated tin box for the humble chamber pot comes from the collection of the West family of Princeton, Massachusetts.*

Antique Tin & Tole Ware ◄❧ 78 ❧►

PLATE 145. *This tin travelling trunk was purchased in England by the author's uncle. It is painted brown on the outside and wagon-wheel blue inside.*

home a brown trunk or box of tin. It must have come from England, for it still has part of a label of a hotel in Liverpool. It is oval in shape, eighteen inches long, a foot wide, and more than a foot deep. It is painted brown with a lovely blue lining. There is a hasp which was fastened with a padlock of some kind. This was my uncle's trunk that held part of his wardrobe. The trunk took the place of a wastebasket beside our Governor Winthrop desk until the value of it was impressed upon me, with its old label and history.

Many of these oval trunk-boxes are found today, most of them are painted with black enamel. They were used to store things in. I bought one at an auction that had a feather boa in it. These boxes belonged to the same period as the oblong tin boxes that had a lock and key. Several of these oblong boxes are in my family, one holding my mother's water-color paints and another with an ances-

tor's name in gold leaf. That period from 1885 to 1895 produced many of these tin utility boxes.

A tin trunk was a practical idea because of its lightness. One such trunk measures twenty-three and one-half inches long, fifteen and one-half inches wide, and seventeen and one-half inches high. It has a flat top that is hinged. Those tin trunks were first used by peddlers when they went from door to door. Alice Morse Earle tells of Chepa Rose, "half Injun, half French and half Yankee," an old-time chapman or peddler who peddled tin trunks. He carried them on his back by means of a hemp webbing, peddling in one section of Rhode Island and eastern Connecticut for at least forty years, previous to 1898. It is doubtful if the trunks were used for travelling because of the liability of being dented. But for large utility trunks there could have been nothing better; the early settlers were wont to save.

The first trunks were made from sections of tree trunks, cut in two and hollowed to make cover and bottom, hinged together.

PLATE 146. *Among the great number of household utensils that were made of tin was the tin bedpan. This one of heavy tin plate looks like pewterware.*

PLATE 147. *Tin was also used on the rims of these wire fly-covers.*

PLATE 148. *This large, round container of tin was made for holding a cheese for market.*

This explains the origin of the name "trunk." These primitive trunks were covered with deerskin or pigskin. Following the log trunks, boxed trunks were made with sides and bottom and a rounded cover made of strips fastened together. Flat-top trunks were made too and probably followed the round-top ones. Round-top trunks might have been easier to pack. The skin covering was fastened with brass nails, and often initials were made with the nails, on top of the cover, sometimes with a date. Hinges, a lock, and handles of rope covered with leather made trunks that could be used when travelling, placed under the seat in the stagecoach. Calfskin might have been used for covering the trunks, but those skins were more valuable as hides for clothing and shoes.

In the days of brick ovens, when food was baked in large quantities and put in the larder to freeze, many pies were stacked one upon another for storage. When tin came into practical use, a tin closet for pies was made in some localities. This practice seems to have originated in Pennsylvania, but like many other things it spread to various parts of the country. "My grandmother came from Pennsylvania and once when she went to her old home to visit, she brought back to Massachusetts many things to lighten her housekeeping," said

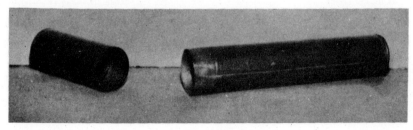

PLATE 149. *This long container of tin is a rare sermon holder of the author's uncle.*

a descendant of my Pennsylvania grandmother, living near Boston. One of those things was a pie closet.

The pie closet was a frame of wood with sides, top, and bottom of sheets of pierced tin, tacked inside the frame. The frame was made of narrow strips of wood, four sides and a center strip, each side fastened to the other side at the edges. The shelves, three or four of them, were of wood. The door was a frame with a sheet of pierced tin fastened on the inside, with hinges and a latch. Some closets hung and some stood on legs and were as much as four feet high and three feet wide and shallow. The purpose of the pierced tin was to allow for the circulation of air and yet to keep out flies and possibly ants. In regard to ants, the pierced holes had to be very small.

This tin closet was patterned after the cheese closet which hung or stood on legs. Cheesecloth was tacked inside the closet frame and this prevented the dreaded cheese fly from getting into the closet while allowing for the circulation of air. Some cheese closets had cheesecloth on the sides, on

PLATE 150. *An array of tin utensils. On the left foreground is a rattle; on the right are a sander and snuffbox.*

Household Utensils of Tin

PLATE 151. *Tin was used to make this mouse trap, another illustration of the many uses that were found for tin.*

the back, and on the door. The closets vary in size according to the need of the family when making cheese. The closet held the cheeses while being cured, buttered, and turned every day until ripe.

In the town of Concord, Massachusetts, the location of many historical events, a tin box for a tricornered hat was found, shaped to fit the hat. Also found there in the Antiquarian Society is a tin box for the gold epaulets that were worn by Union officers in the Civil War. The box is lined with red satin and has the name of the maker inside the lid.

Tin toys began to be made by 1880. They came in great numbers and brought much joy to children. There were tin stoves, fully equipped with tiny utensils, and tin stores with counters and all the things that were found in real stores, made of tin and painted in gay colors. Soldiers, animals, carts—the list is long, and many are found in museums today.

An unusual piece of tinware is an astronomical lantern. This was made by Lock-wood, Brooks Co., 381 Washington Street, Boston and bears the date of 1878. The one in the illustration is owned by the Society for the Preservation of New England Antiquities in Boston, and probably there are other such lanterns in and around Boston. The idea for such a lantern was patented in 1870.

The lantern is about twelve inches long and is semicircular in shape. It is japanned tin with gold lines around the edges and around the door at the back, with a design on the one handle. The front side, that is the flat side, has two grooves, one of which holds a piece of ground glass and the other, in front of the glass, a chart of the heavens. The charts are light blue like the sky, and the constellations are outlined in white, each star having been pricked to allow the light to show through. There are seventeen charts, covering the entire range of the heavens.

Within the lantern, behind the ground glass and charts, are holders for four candles. When these were lighted, the light rays penetrated through the pricked holes, and, as one held the lantern in the right hand, the constellations on the charts could be seen clearly. At the right-hand end of each

PLATES 153 & 154. *Two views of an astronomical lantern made in 1872. Charts showing the constellations were placed in the front and were illuminated from the back by a pair of candles.*

chart is a description of the constellation shown. A booklet accompanies the lantern, titled *How to Find the Stars* and with an account by James Freeman Clarke on "The Astronomical Lantern and Its Use."

In my home, many years ago, there was a globe made of blue paper showing the entire heavens. Each star and constellation was pricked and labelled with its name. When using it, you held it up to the light so as to see the pricked stars. It was given to the family by a Clark University professor and was a rare means of informative education, of which we children took ad-

PLATE 152. *In the Concord Antiquarian Society is this container for the golden epaulets worn by a Union officer during the Civil War.*

vantage. Being made of paper, in the course of the years, it became torn and was thrown away.

A chapter on tin should mention the magic lantern which threw pictures onto a screen. A lamp produced the light in back of a lens, and a holder between the lamp and the lens held the slides. We had many slides in color in our family; they came in sets depicting a series of actions. The slides moved along, four pictures in each slide. It was most exciting in those days to follow these moving slides.

The ubiquitous tin can is a humble object, but surely a note about its origin and early history is not out of place in a discussion of the role tinware played in the household.

In a small book titled *Historic Tinned Foods* put out by the International Tin Research and Development Council of Middlesex, England, the origin of tin cans holding perishable foods is fully discussed. It was in 1806 that Nicholas Appert of France began experimenting with sealing food in glass bottles. His theory was that "contact with air is the chief cause of putrefaction." A year later, Bryan Donkin, acclaimed the

PLATE 155. *Also in the Concord Antiquarian Society is found this tin box for the tricornered hat worn by soldiers of the American Revolution.*

father of the modern canning industry, began experimenting with iron containers. Augustur de Heine and Peter Durand took out patents for the use of iron and tin containers.

The food thus canned included meats, soup, flour, oatmeal, raisins, sugar, cocoa, butter, cheese, lemon juice, and stews. Such supplies were taken on the ships "Isabella" and "Alexander" to Baffin Bay as early as 1814. The list of meats was long. The word

PLATE 156. *Nearly thirty years ago these tin articles were made for a tin anniversary. From the Keillor collection of Wading River, Long Island.*

PLATE 157. *A leader pipe of tin made to join two pipes of different dimensions. Note the unusual workmanship in the decorations. From the New York Historical Society of Cooperstown, New York.*

bouilli was attached to some of the cans of meats. This became "bully-beef" as the seamen attempted to pronounce the name of this foreign dish. The word is of French origin and means beef and vegetables boiled in water.

The cans were made of tin plate. Here again in this small book, it is stated that wrought iron was refined with both charcoal and coke. Charcoal was in time given up in favor of coke. The cans were made in England, and the tin plate came from South Wales or Cornwall. A can was made in Chicago in 1880 from tin supplied by South Wales. This would suggest that there were no tin-plate manufactories in the United States at that time.

Some of those earliest cans of food have been preserved and from these much has been learned of the making of the cans and of the contents. All ships eventually carried canned food, which was more popular than the dried foods of earlier days.

Many more articles of tin have not been included in this chapter. Every locality produced and used a great variety of tinware which helped to lighten the burdens of the housewife and made the home a brighter and happier place.

CHAPTER FOUR

A Light after Dark

ORKING from sunup until sundown was the usual routine in the days of our forefathers. Providing shelter, food, and clothing was an exacting task, and those pioneers became hardy as they struggled and made new frontiers.

After sundown, the question of a light by which to continue some of the household duties brought into use a natural resource in the form of pine-wood pitch. When trees were cut down to make space for a new settlement, the wood was used for household furnishings, kitchen equipment, and for firewood. The Indians taught this wood lore to the new white settlers, as they taught them other important ways of living.

Perhaps the Indians taught the white men that pitch in slivers of wood from the pine trees and in the pine knots in the dead trees could give a light for the home. Or perhaps those pioneers watched sap and pitch ooze from the burning logs on the hearth and saw a tiny flame burn and flicker like a candlelight. However it may have been, splinters of pine were cut and used as the

first means of making a light after dark. Those splinters were called candlewood and were gathered in the fall of the year along with nuts which were stored for the winter and oak leaves which were used in the deep ovens as a floor on which to place the loaves of bread and, last but not least, the corn shucks which were used to fill mattresses. The splinters were stuck into crevices in the chimney, dripping onto the hearth as they burned. Or they were placed in pincer-like holders of various sorts, made of wood or of iron.

At the same time that candlewood was gathered in the fall of the year, pine knots were taken from dead trees that had fallen. The knots were sometimes burned lying on the hearth, but holders were made for them by the village blacksmith and these were called cressets or firebaskets. One such holder was in the shape of an urn on a base, made of iron bands with uprights holding them in position. Many families knew only the light of the blazing logs and those flickering pine knots. History relates that many a sermon or famous work were thus written and that pioneer families and their children, including that of Abraham Lincoln, read and studied by such insufficient light as was provided by burning pine knots.

A type of andiron brought from England had a basket cup at the top of the upright, in which a pine knot could be placed for more light than what came from the blazing logs. These holders on the andirons were also used to hold a basting cup while the roasts were turned and basted on a spit that rested on brackets attached to the uprights of the andirons. And even mugs of hot toddy were set into these holders to be kept warm between long draughts of the host and his guests.

The pine knot was found to provide sufficient light when hunting or fishing at nighttime. For outdoor use another form of cresset was made of iron bands set together in the shape of a backbone and ribs, some having a top band and others none. These basket holders were commonly about two or three feet long, with a short iron arm extending from the center rod, bent at right angles and held in a long handle. The handle was stuck into the ground, and the basket holding the knot was in a horizontal position. The light from these pine

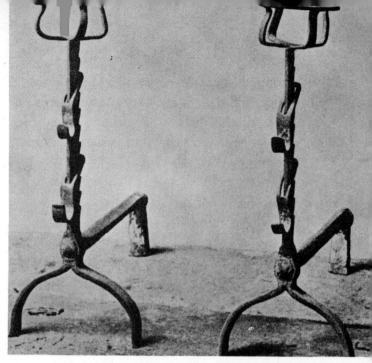

PLATE 160. *These interesting hand-wrought andirons brought from England had toddy-cup holders at the top. Also note the adjustable brackets for spit rods. From the collection of Gertrude Jekyl.*

knots attracted deer and other wild animals when the colonists went hunting in the deep woods. When used for fishing, the handle of the cresset was fastened to the end of the boat, the knot casting its flickering light upon the water.

In later years, when hunting suckers in the streams at nighttime, a lamp swinging on a pole was used. The lamp had two burners and used sperm oil for fuel. With the pole of the lamp in one hand and a

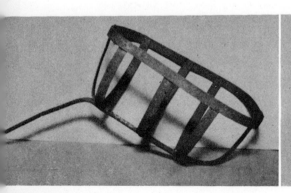

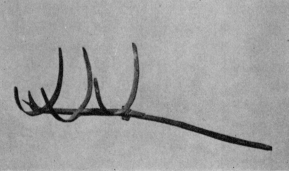

PLATES 158 & 159. *Pine knots were one of the first means used by the colonists to provide light. For outdoor use cressets like these were made to hold the burning pine knots.*

Antique Tin & Tole Ware ❦ 86 ❦

pronged spear on a wooden handle in the other, the men waded through streams and speared the fish when they came upon them. This type of lamp was also used in torchlight processions.

The burning of some form of oil for light dates back to the beginning of mankind. A commonly-known holder for oil was made of iron, called a Betty lamp, and such a type was brought to the new land. History relates that Captain John Carver, first Governor of the Plymouth Colony, bought such a lamp in Holland before he set sail on the "Mayflower."

PLATE 162. *Swinging lamps were attached to the ends of poles for fishing at night or for torchlight processions. This torch is from the Stone House of Belchertown, Massachusetts.*

PLATE 161. *An elaborate Betty lamp was made of tin and was attached to a stand. From the collection of Isabel Gordon.*

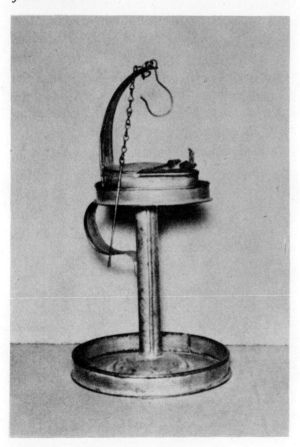

This early Betty lamp was a rounded, shallow, covered holder with a long, open snout protruding from the front. A narrow holder was fastened in the trough of the snout, where the wick rested, drawing oil from the main reservoir. The holder was tilted and a space was left for the drippings, which went back again into the reservoir. The trough was open and over it a narrow cover pivoted on a pin, having a tiny projection for a knob. When the wick was burning, the slide was closed to make a draft for the flame.

At the back of the Betty lamp is an extending curved arm about six inches long. Into a hole at the end, a chain four inches long was fastened. At the end of the chain is an arm about five inches long, pointed at the tip with a right-angle hook projecting near the end. The entire lamp was hand-wrought. The point could be jabbed into the wooden lintel of the hearth or in a crevice of the stones or bricks. And the point was used when picking out the wick as it burned or became crusted. The hook was used when the lamp was hung on the back of a settle or of a chair. The early Bettys had only one chain and arm, while later ones had two extensions, a hook

PLATE 163. *On the left is a typical early Betty lamp. The pick at the end of the chain was jabbed into the lintel over the fireplace to hold the lamp and was also used to freshen the wick. On the right is an unusual double cruse that could have been used as one lamp, one inside the other, or as two separate lamps.*

by which the lamp was hung and a chain with a long pick on the end. The pick in both types was used not only to jab into the wooden lintel but also to freshen the wick.

A double cruse or phoebe is in my museum, different from the ordinary type because the two parts are the same size and the upright has no hook on which the inner part hung. The inner one has a short upright with a finial of three curves. This part could have been used as a separate lamp with a separate wick, or the two parts could have been placed together and one wick used. There is no place for the oil to drip so when used as two separate lamps, something must have been placed beneath to catch the drip. In the common Betty, the inner cup hangs on the upright of the outer cup and the wick was placed in the inner, dripping over into the outer.

Oil for lamps was obtained at first from the fish found along the coast. Most of the early towns were located by the sea for

navigating purposes and because of the abundance of fish, mostly cod, which provided both food and oil for light. The whaling industry brought another oil to the homes, that from the sperm whale. Within the head of the whale is a large pocket containing fluid oil and a granulated substance which yields spermaceti. This sperm was used in lamps, and the waxy spermaceti was used for candles. The whaling industry was a colorful part in the lives of several generations of early settlers, entailing many risks as well as offering intense excitement to the men engaged in it. It brought much wealth to their families.

The history of the progress of lamps is not for such a book as this. Beginning with the Betty lamps, the types were many, each with their names, made of iron, tin, pewter, pottery, glass, and china. Those of tin were

PLATE 164. *The peculiar device on the left is a vapor lamp with a small oil burner. It was used to administer vapor treatments to asthma patients. The cup with the hinged lid on the right was used for warming rum.*

Antique Tin & Tole Ware ❧ 88 ❧

numerous and are well worth collecting. A group is illustrated, belonging to the museum. At the left is a type used on a whaling vessel, having a large, round wick in a round head and an opening with a cork stopper into which oil was poured. This stands about eight inches high and is very sturdy, as things used on whaling vessels had to be. The long lamp in the center with three capped wicks has been called a guest lamp for no logical reason whatsoever, a point which should be proved. Sometimes these had four bracket feet and a handle at one side. Next to this is one that hung on the wall, with three tiny wicks in the front extension and at the back an opening with a screw cap for the oil. At the right is a tin lamp with a brass screw cap, holding four slender wicks, which would make more light than one, two, or three. This was brought to my door by a lawyer who had taken it in lieu of money when he helped an elderly lady with some legal business.

The two round boxed lamps resemble the tinderbox which has a socket for a candle.

PLATE 166. *After the Betty lamps, a wide variety of lamps were developed. Some had a number of wicks, and their styles were many. The lamp on the extreme left was used on a whaling vessel, while the lamp in the center with a back was hung on the wall.*

These have three wicks. The first three lamps described have openings for oil to be poured in, and the last three are merely holders with wicks extending from the oil inside the holders. There are other tin lamps such as the petticoat lamp with a skirt, the lamps on saucers, those with long heads and flat wicks, those hanging, those with and without reflectors—all of them made in many shapes and having various names in different localities.

From fish oil, whale oil, and lard oil, the burning fluids for lamps passed to petroleum, camphene, and kerosene. Petroleum was found by 1814, dug from wells. When used in its crude form it was dark and thick, making a smoky flame. After it was distilled it became kerosene. Lamps burning kerosene are still used today, partly because their use became a habit and partly because remote sections have no other means of obtaining light. Camphene was a variety of spirit of turpentine and was used only for a short time, because of its danger of

PLATE 165. *Oil for the lamps was kept easily accessible in containers like these two. The one on the right is a very early model and was used for whale oil.*

PLATE 167. *This hand-some lamp is made of brass and has an exceptional shade made of sections of molded tin.*

PLATE 169. *This quaint lamp from the collection of the Hosmer family of Lancaster, Massachusetts shows rather unusual workmanship in the way the shade is attached to the body of the lamp.*

PLATE 168. *This tin chimney for a lamp has a small hole covered with isinglass on the side and was used in the sickroom.*

exploding. The vapor formed with air was a very explosive mixture.

Two small cans came to my museum while I was writing about oil for lamps. They were found in an old barn. One can stands six inches high and is very early, having a handle at the side of the can. The other is seven inches high and still holds some thick, dark-colored oil, presumably petroleum. Such small cans were kept at hand, filled with oil, ready for the daily task of filling the lamps. The early can has a tin cap, while the other one has an old cork stopper.

Kerosene lamps brought another era into the homes. My adopted grandmother said when her father brought home some kerosene in the middle of the nineteenth century, there was great rejoicing. The lamps burning kerosene were many, having a broad, flat wick that was woven of cotton. Pewter, glass, china, and brass lamps were made in many attractive and beautiful shapes. Many

Antique Tin & Tole Ware ❧ 90 ❧

wall lamps with reflectors held kerosene, and both single lamps and chandeliers appeared in churches and in public buildings.

The history of lanterns makes another interesting chapter in lighting. Various oils were used for the burners in the lanterns, although many still used candles. The kerosene lanterns are used today in many sections and in various ways. The one lantern known to all collectors seems to be the so-called Paul Revere lantern. It was made of pierced tin, cylindrical in shape with a conical top, and was carried by a large ring. This burned a candle. Paul Revere, as is generally known, was a tin-smith as well as a silversmith and because he made tin trays, he doubtless fashioned these tin lanterns. History tells us that one lantern was swung from the Old North Church in Boston to signal Paul Revere at the time of the approach of the British by land, and collectors have naturally connected the pierced lantern with that event. The fact that the rays of light coming

PLATE 171. *This is the celebrated "Paul Revere lantern" that was swung from the steeple of the Old North Church to signal the approach of the British by land. Concord Anti-quarian Society.*

PLATE 170. *This is an example of the standard railroad lamp that was used on the early railroads.*

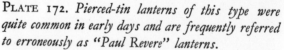

PLATE 172. *Pierced-tin lanterns of this type were quite common in early days and are frequently referred to erroneously as "Paul Revere" lanterns.*

PLATE 173. *This early tin lantern has a beautifully shaped glass globe with tin top and base.*

PLATE 175. *This lantern of tin is only six inches high and has a red and green glass inside that could be turned by twisting the conical cap, thus switching the color of the light.*

PLATE 174. *A sturdy tin lantern with glass windows. It burned whale oil in a square tin burner.*

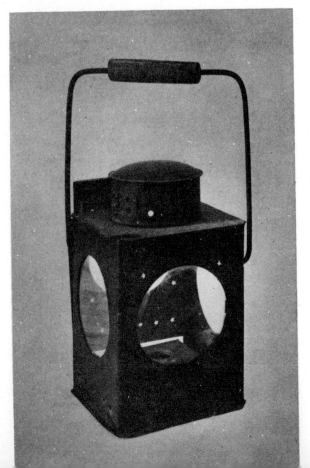

through the holes of such a lantern were quite dim proves to the historian that Paul Revere was never signaled by such a lantern from the church steeple, although he well could have made such a lantern.

The lantern rightly accredited to that event had four glass sides, from which a maximum amount of light could shine. It was made with a tin frame, corner posts with finials, and two small cylinders on the top cut in the manner of the panels of the tin foot stoves, which acted as ventilators. A ring above these cylinders was used in carrying or hanging the lantern. Paul Revere's lantern, shown here, now hangs in the Concord Antiquarian Society of Concord, Massachusetts.

The early lanterns using candles were made with wooden or tin frames and with glass panels, one side being the door. There were many shapes, and a tinsmith was the creator. Two other lanterns are in the museum, one round with a glass lamp and the other square with a square tin lamp, both burning oil.

Lanterns developed in the same manner

Antique Tin & Tole Ware ❦| 92 |❧

as did lamps. Whale oil and candles were both used, with kerosene following. In spite of the fact that electricity lights the world today, lanterns made serviceable and safe are still found, serving their purpose in many ways.

A primitive means of lighting was the rushlight. Rushes in the salt marshes were at first used for thatch on the roofs of the houses of the early settlers, following the custom of using thatch in the old country. Lots of rush marshes were assigned to each village inhabitant, each one having a certain amount. When taking rushes for thatch, some were set aside for rushlights, another custom carried over from old England.

The rushes were stripped of their outer covering, and the long pith was dipped in tallow or grease and then hung to harden. These made long tapers, as the illustration shows. In the lean years, deer suet, bear's grease, moose fat, or coon or possum fat was clarified and used as tallow in which to dip the rushes. A rare iron grease holder

PLATES 177 & 178. *These are two examples of rushlight holders. The loop on the model on the right acted as a spring to hold the pith, while on the other a pincer arrangement with a weight is used. It is shown with a paper spill.*

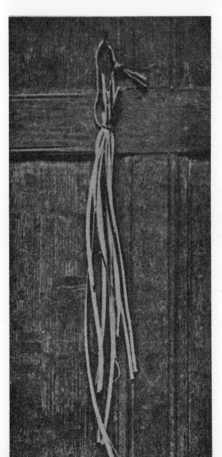

PLATE 176. *Rushes were stripped of their outer covering, and the long piths were dipped in tallow and hung to harden before they were used as rushlights. The rushes shown are from the collection of Gertrude Jekyl.*

PLATE 179. *This tripod of iron came from England and was used to hold the tallow for dipping the rushes. From the collection of James A. Keillor.*

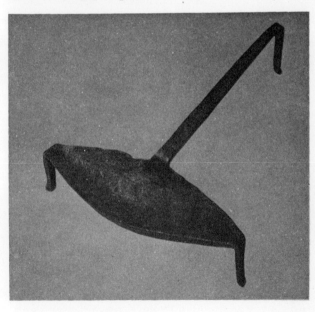

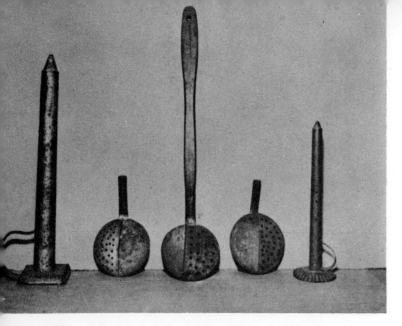

PLATE 180. *The melted animal fats had to be skimmed of impurities before they could be used for making candles. Tallow scoops like these shown here with two candle molds were used for that purpose. They were made both for left-handed and right-handed use.*

used for dipping rushes that was brought over from England is shown. Holders for these rushes were made like iron pincers set into a base of wood or iron. The dipped rush was held between the jaws and, as it burned, it was moved along. Some holders were combined with a socket for one candle. A rare tin rushlight holder is shown.

A substitute for dipped rushes was a paper or wood spill. A piece of paper was wound diagonally around a knitting needle, the entire length. Then the needle was drawn out, and the ends of the spill were turned up to keep it from unwinding. Many of these were made and kept near the fireplace ready to use, hanging in a paper cornucopia. Wood spills were made by shaving the side of a pine board less than an inch in thickness. As the wood was shaved, it curled of itself. The ends were sometimes dipped in tallow to seal them. These paper and wood spills were burned in rush holders, one such

paper spill is shown. The museum boasts of both paper and wood spills.

Records show that candles were made and used in the sixteenth century. But they were not made in the new land for many years. Alice Morse Earle tells that when Governor Winthrop arrived in Massachusetts, he promptly wrote to his wife to bring candles with her from England when she came. And in 1634, he sent over for a large quantity of wicks and tallow, showing that tallow was a little known commodity in the new land.

When domestic animals increased, and sheep and cows were killed for the meat as well as for their pelts and hides, all the fat was saved and this was the beginning of making candles in greater numbers. Wicks were made from the coarse part of flax called tow and spun on the flax wheel, and sometimes, if this was not to be had, milkweed fibre was spun into wicks.

Fat was clarified in a big iron kettle hanging on the crane in the fireplace or perhaps outdoors over a fire. Sliced potatoes were sometimes used when clarifying, because of the starch in them. The melted fat was skimmed of all impurities with a tin tallow scoop and at times strained through cheesecloth. There were two scaldings and two skimmings. The scoop had a round head, a solid back section and a perforated half section soldered in front, both parts concave. There is a left-handed one in the illustration and two right-handed ones. One has a long wooden handle and the other two, short handles of tin. The clear melted tallow was put into a large kettle half filled with boiling water, ready for the dipping process. Sometimes two kettles were used if a great number of candles were to be made.

Candles were hand-dipped in the early days. This work was done in the fall of the year after the hot summer had passed, so the candles might harden more quickly. While the tallow was being kept hot in the kettles on the crane, the tow wicks were made. Some housewives used a nine-inch board to wind the tow on, making as many loops as the board would hold. Then the tow was cut at the edge of the board, and each piece measured eighteen inches long, ready to be twisted over the candle rods.

There is hardly an old attic that does not have a bundle of candle rods, some long and some short, tied together with a stout cord. These were slender sticks of birch or poplar wood, polished to a fine smoothness. The long rods measured about eighteen inches and the short ones a few inches less. Two long rods rested on the backs of two

PLATE 182. *A bundle of old candle rods are shown here with two early tin candleholders. These were called "hog-back" candleholders, because their bases were often used to scrape the bristles from the backs of hogs.*

chairs, placed back to back, and six or eight short rods were placed across these two. On each short rod, the strands of tow were twisted. A strand was looped over the rod with the fingers, first dipped in tallow, the better to hold the strand as it was twisted. This made a twisted strand a little less than nine inches long, about the length of a finished candle. When all the strands were twisted on all the rods, there were thirty-six or forty-eight of them. With eight rods and eight strands, sixty-four candles were made at one time. A skillful housewife could make as many as forty dozen candles in a day's work.

From these sticks that lay across the backs of two chairs, comes the old nursery rhyme:

Jack be nimble, Jack be quick;
Jack jump over the candle stick.

The kettle was swung out into the room and the dipping began. Because of the

PLATE 181. *Slender rods of birch or poplar were used as candle rods to hang the wicks before dipping them in tallow. After the rods were dipped they were suspended across the backs of chairs.*

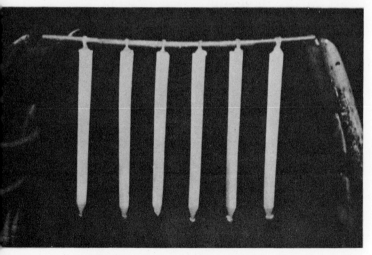

uncomfortable heat of the great fire, the kettles were sometimes taken to the end of the kitchen or into the lean-to, the workroom back of the kitchen. One rod of wicks was dipped into the kettle, put into place again, another rod was dipped and put back, and so on until all of the six or eight rods were dipped. Beginning with the first one again, which had slightly hardened, the process was repeated. Each time, more tallow clung to the candle, and it began to take shape. Finally, the candles were of the right size and the dipping ceased. They naturally tapered as the tallow dripped off the tip into a pan on the floor, to be saved and returned to the kettle. During the dipping the kettle of tallow had to be reheated once or twice, as it hardened very quickly and nothing was more disappointing to a housewife than to have candles that were not perfectly smooth.

Within fifteen or twenty minutes, the

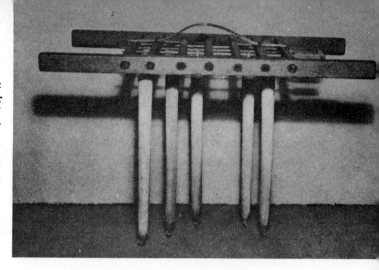

PLATE 184. *Special holders were made for holding the candles while they were hardening. From the collection of Mrs. Nina Fletcher Little.*

candles were hard enough to slide off the rods. They were smoothed of any imperfections. Many were the ways by which the candles were hung to finish drying. One contrivance in the collection of Mrs. Nina Fletcher Little is shown. A frame was made with two wide sidepieces and seven smaller crosspieces. Running through holes made in the small crosspieces, slender rods were set, marking off thirty-six squares. The slender rods have long heads and could be pulled out of the frame when the candles were to be strung onto them, through their loops. Thirty-six candles could be hung in the frame at one time, suspended from an overhead beam.

Another invention that was commonly used was the hickory branch. From a small center twig, several smaller twigs branched out, which, when cut off short, resembled a small hat tree. Onto each branch, a candle was hung. These hickory twigs could easily have been made just before the time for candle-dipping and probably there were many of them.

A wooden box with a sliding cover with

PLATE 183. *When the candles had hardened enough to be stored, they were kept in wooden boxes like the one shown here to prevent them from turning yellow under exposure.*

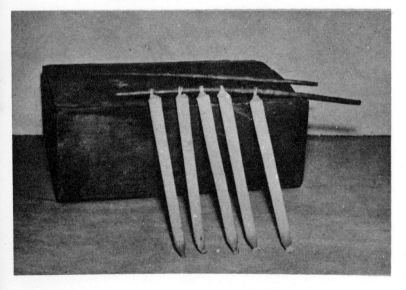

finger notches was used to store candles in, away from the light and the mice and in a cool place, preferably in the cellar. Such a box is pictured, which was found filled with candles, two long candle rods, and a few short ones. The candles had been pared and smoothed of any imperfections, but the loops were still on. This type of box with a sliding cover was used when candles were peddled by peddlers. Filled with candles, the box weighed about forty pounds. To weigh the box and candles, a special platform was made with one arm and this was hung on a steelyard.

A handy invention made to assist in the labor of dipping candles by hand was a turnstile. This has a base, a standard two feet high, and six or eight arms extending from the hub, like spokes of a wheel. The arms revolve around the standard. At the end of each arm is a round thin board, swinging by a hook. On the under part of each board are six or eight hooks. Onto each hook, a tow wick was looped and twisted, twice the length of the finished candle. When dipping, a kettle of hot tallow was swung out from the fire, and a board

PLATE 185. *Some of the candles were kept near at hand for immediate use in candleboxes of tin. These were usually hung near the fireplace.*

with its wicks was dipped into it. Lifted, the board was moved on, and a second arm was dipped. Each arm was revolved and dipped until all the candles were completed. This contrivance eliminated much lifting that was necessary when candle rods were used, and more candles could be dipped in much less time.

The commonly known candleholder is the long tin box, with two extensions at the back by which it hung and a cover that lifted with a hasp. These measure about fourteen inches long. A few candles were taken from the wooden box, trimmed of the loop, and put into the tin candlebox, which hung near the fireplace, but away from the heat, either high on the wooden mantel or on the jamb at the side. Enough candles were kept in the box at all times to replenish those that had burned out in an evening. One candle lasted about four hours.

Tin candleholders were the first to be made in this country, the early type with a saucer and a loop handle and a lip at the top edge of the holder. Inside the opening was a small lift that was controlled by a lip outside; as the candle burned, the lift could be raised and more candle length supplied. Some holders were made with an inverted base and these acquired the name of "hog scrapers," because they were handy when scraping bristles off the scalded hog. Some of the holders did not have a lip at the top edge. But with a lip the candle could be hung on the rung of a chair back or on the back of a settle, giving light, even though feeble, when reading.

Before tin appeared in the homes, candleholders were of brass, brought over from

PLATE 186. *Two early tin candleholders are shown here with a group of snuffers and pickwicks. The snuffer on the left is of tin, whereas the pickwick and snuffer in the center are made of wood. To the right of them is an unusual combination wick-trimmer and snuffer of steel on a beautifully decorated tin tray.*

the old country. These are very beautiful in shape and design and prized by collectors and owners. Silver and pewter ones were made by whitesmiths and silversmiths. Candelabras, or several arms with holders, were very popular, made in silver or brass. The brass ones were elaborately made in sets of three, one a large central part and two smaller side parts. The standards often had a figure holding the arms which held the candles. These had hanging crystals and, all told, were very ornate, decorating homes of elegance in the times of prosperity.

It has aptly been said that "necessity is the mother of invention." Two things were made when candles were in use, one a pickwick and the other a snuffer. Pickwicks are rarely found and little known. My first one was of copper, which is now in Old Sturbridge Village, Sturbridge, Massachusetts. My second one is of wood and will always remain in my collection. The idea

of the pickwick was to have a sharp point to pick up the wick if it drooped or sputtered. The head of the pickwick is a handle with a steel pin inserted in it. This sets, inverted, into the short standard. The whole piece is not more than three inches high. Pickwicks are so seldom seen that they are not recognized as early inventions very necessary in the days of candles. My adopted grandmother told of picking up the wicks with a pin to make a brighter flame.

Snuffers were created to snuff out a candle and prevent tallow from spilling if blown out. Tin snuffers were for the tin candleholders, made like a dunce cap, with a tiny loop handle. One snuffer was found made of wood, now in the museum. One conical one was made of copper, at the end of a long handle, used to snuff out candles hanging in chandeliers. A decorative snuffer was made of steel. It has pincer-like scissors with one pointed end to pick up the wick.

Antique Tin & Tole Ware ❧ 98 ☙

Near the end is a box on one arm and a flat piece fitting into the box on the other arm. This was the part that snuffed the flame. The snuffers had three short legs or feet and were found with a tray on which they rested. Many tin snuffer trays are beautifully decorated in dainty patterns. Sometimes a drop of turpentine was put onto the wick. Candles were not as hard to care for as lamps, which needed to be filled regularly.

An unusual find was a tin candle shield, standing much higher than a candle in a holder. It could have been used not only for a shield but also as a reflector to make more light.

The idea of intensifying the candle light brought about reflectors. They were used when a candleholder was hung on a wall. Many interesting reflectors are found, in-

PLATE 188. *A number of candle shields were made to reflect and intensify the light of the candles. This simple shield is rather rare of its kind.*

cluding the plain ones with fluted edges and those elaborate ones with glass insertions, mostly round, a few elliptical or oblong. They were concave, the better to diffuse the light. In the chandelier which hung on a whaling vessel and is described later, the four holders for the candles each have a round convex reflector. This would disperse the light over a wider range than a reflector that was concave. The candles that had reflectors behind them were called sconces and hung on walls, in homes, in public halls, and in churches. In the museum is a pair of tin sconces that were once used in the Allen Evangelical Church of Dedham, Massachusetts, previous to 1820. It is typical of those used in homes and churches at that time, with long, slender backs, and a fluted, curved top.

Lamps had reflectors behind them when they hung, of tin and of glass, the tin often silvered to make for more reflection. But the earliest reflector was the bull's-eye glass.

PLATE 187. *When the Continental Congress met at Carpenter's Hall in Philadelphia in 1775, the hall was lit by candle sconces with mirror reflectors. This is one of the original sconces, twenty-four inches high.*

These appeared by the middle of the eighteenth century. They were added to pewter lamps that burned whale oil, and only one bull's-eye was used at first; the thin extension of the holder of the eye slipped into a flat holder at one side of the lamp. Sometimes there was a holder on either side of the lamp for two bull's-eyes.

When tinsmiths began to make tinware, giving housewives many helpful additions for their work, tin candle molds were made. The long and difficult job of dipping candles by hand changed to one of pouring tallow into molds. Many molds are still found, for making candles continued well into the beginning of the twentieth century. These are often used today as candelabras, for decorative purposes. The candle mold was the shape of a dipped candle, tapering toward the tip. It was made with a frame at the top and bottom with rims around the edge and a handle to hold the frame when pouring the tallow. Single molds and those of two or three were sometimes made with no base, the ends of the molds soldered together.

The tin mold most commonly used was for twelve candles. There were single molds,

PLATE 190. *Molds arranged in circular fashion like these two examples were rather rare. These come from the collection of W. S. Redhed of Champaign, Illinois.*

PLATE 191. *The three molds in the center are of standard size. The large molds were probably used for making altar candles.*

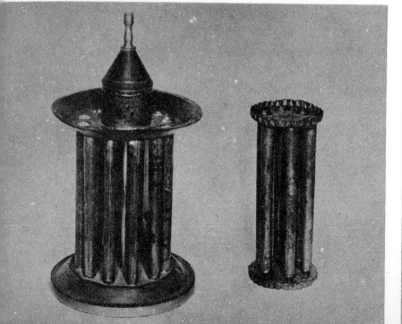

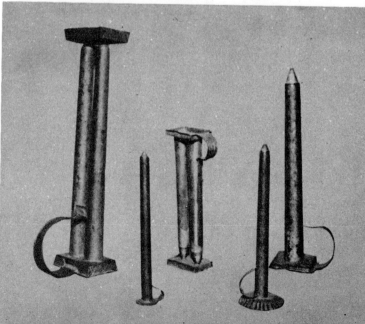

those for two candles, those for three, four, six, one dozen, two dozen, six dozen, and eight dozen. One unusual mold for two dozen was set in a circular top and bottom. Two molds, standing twenty inches high, were used for altar candles, one single and one double. An early mold in the museum, illustrated, has pewter molds for three dozen candles set in a wooden frame with wooden sides extending beyond the top of the molds, like a box. Other wooden frames were made to hold one or two dozen molds. Some were made of pewter, others of tin and Bennington pottery, sometimes white and sometimes mottled.

In a town near Worcester lives a man who is the third of a generation of candle and soap makers. His grandfather, born in 1808, began the business, peddling his products in surrounding towns. He used molds in wooden frames, three dozen in each frame. I purchased his last frame, many of the others having been burned up as junk. Across the top of each row is a wire,

PLATE 193. *A very early mold with thirty-six tubes of pewter. The scraper on the left was used to scrape off the excess tallow that overflowed into the boxlike top of the wooden frame.*

running through the top side walls, over which the wicks were looped. With a slender, shaped stick, the wick was pushed down into the mold and then knotted at the tip. The tallow was poured in with a pail having a broad, flat snout. The side walls of the frame kept the tallow from running over. Any surplus tallow was scraped up with the wooden scraper that has a wedge-shaped head with a sharp end and was put back into the kettle. I purchased my friend's slender stick that pushed in the wicks, the scraper, and the frame on which the tow was wound, all having been saved from being burned as junk. The frame has a razor blade set in at one end and a peg at the other, eight inches apart. The tow was wound around as many times as the blade would hold. Then the loops were sawed against the blade, which cut them. Each strand was sixteen inches long, which when doubled

PLATE 192. *This homemade wooden frame was used to cut the tow. It rested on the knees, and the tow was wound around the pole on the left and the razor blade on the right. This cut the tow in even lengths.*

over the candle rod made one eight-inch candlewick. The frame rested on the knees when it was being used. Pictured also is a tallow pourer with three snouts, which made an easier job of pouring the tallow. Some pourers have as many as five snouts.

The story of making candles in molds has been beautifully told by L. M. A. Roy of Henniker, New Hampshire, who lives in the Ocean-born Mary House. The house was so named because of the fact that its first mistress had been born on board ship, crossing the Atlantic. Mr. Roy is a photographer of no mean reputation and he took pictures of his mother, then living, making candles, step by step. The book is titled *The Candle Book*. The mother was garbed in a voluminous skirt, a kerchief over her shoulders, and a lace cap on her head, tied under her chin. Her gnarled hands show that she had toiled all the days of her life, keeping house for her family, as women did in those early years.

The tallow was strained through cheesecloth as well as being skimmed. Tallow of beef suet was preferred. The candle wicking was loosely spun cotton or tow, with four or six strands twisted into one wick. Some-

PLATE 195. *This unusual tin scoop was used for pouring tallow into candle molds. From the collection of W. S. Redhed of Champaign, Illinois.*

times, the wick was threaded up and down through the molds or again down each mold and tied in a knot at the tip. A short wooden stick or a wire skewer held the loop over each mold as it was threaded and tied. A tin mold in my museum was found strung, ready for the tallow, mute evidence that the housewife was obliged to leave her job unfinished. In this case, a knot was tied at the end of each mold.

The tallow was poured in with a tin cup; one such cup is in my museum. It took from fifteen minutes to half an hour for the tallow to harden. Then the loops or knots were cut at the bottom, and the mold quickly dipped into hot water to loosen the tallow from the sides. Then, when the wooden skewer or wire was lifted, the candles came out easily with no bruises. They were hung down cellar to harden, which took four or five days. Stored in wooden candleboxes such as the one shown in the book, they were kept from the light, which turned the tallow yellow. When thoroughly hardened, a few at a time were taken out, the loops

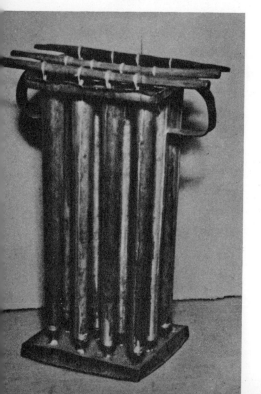

PLATE 194. *This early tin mold was found completely ready for the pouring of the tallow. The strands of tow had been looped over the candle rods and tied at the bottom of the frame to keep them taut.*

Antique Tin & Tole Ware ❧ 102 ❧

cut off, and they were put into the tin candle-box that hung not far from the fireplace, ready to be used.

Housewives were considered shiftless if they made only a few candles at one time. The thrifty housewife made a large batch in the fall, either dipping them or pouring the tallow into molds. Alice Morse Earle says that if the room was fairly cool, a good worker could dip two hundred candles in one day, dipping two rods at a time. With many candle molds, several dozen candles each, the operation was faster and many more could be done in less time. A Herculean job!

Many times, the job of making candles was turned over to an itinerant candle-maker. He went from house to house, carrying his own molds. In return for his work, the candlemaker was given lodging and meals, his "board and keep." Board came from the table board on which food was served. And he was often given fat or suet

PLATE 197. *Candles were often made from beeswax. This set of square molds, however, is said to have been used for making beeswax cakes for the seamstress to use in her sewing.*

or even tallow to take away with him, which he made into candles which he bartered for commodities for himself.

Farmers kept bees for the honey and for wax. Honey was used as sweetening before the coming of sugar, and the wax was used in making dipped candles. Rushlights, too, were dipped in beeswax and another use for this wax was to make small cakes for the seamstress to use in her sewing. A mold is shown, said to have been used in making beeswax cakes.

A fragrant wax was obtained from the bayberry bush. The bush grew in great profusion along the coast and in pastures, and the early settlers used the berry for its wax, having known about the bush in the old country. In Sweden, it was called the tallow shrub, while in England it was called the candleberry tree or bayberry bush. The berries were gathered late in the autumn and put into a kettle of boiling water. The wax came to the surface and was skimmed off and put into another kettle. It took one bushel of berries to make four or five pounds of wax to use in candles. The candles were found to be far superior

PLATE 196. *Simple tin cups like this were also used frequently for pouring the tallow.*

PLATE 198. *This very unusual chandelier hung in the captain's cabin of a whaling vessel.*

to those of tallow or beeswax, because they did not bend, they burned slower and brighter, and they made no smoke. The odor of the burning bayberry candle was like incense, so fragrant and refreshing it was. The gathering of bayberries became so important that a law was passed in Long Island that berries could not be picked until September 15th, under penalty of a fine. This was as early as 1687, before tallow from animals had become a common household commodity.

At the time when sperm oil was taken from the sperm whale, spermaceti was taken and sold for use in making candles. It was said that a candle made from spermaceti wax gave as much light as three tallow candles and a flame four times as large. The manu-

facture of these candles increased, and although they cost more than the ordinary candles, they were a great improvement over them.

For a good number of years the whaling industry was one of the most important and lucrative of the industries on the coast of New England. The oil, the spermaceti, the whalebone, the ambergris, the bones that were carved, and the blubber, all made the industry a means of great wealth to the owner of whaling vessels. Nantucket and New Bedford were both whaling centers. The beautiful homes of the Georgian type, with their elaborate furnishings and social life were the result of the wealth that came at the time of the prosperous era of the whaling industry.

The oil obtained from the head of the sperm whale or from the blubber of any of the other whales was used for lamps; the spermaceti was used in making candles,

PLATE 199. *Miner's candleholders were often used in the home, jabbed into the lintel over the fireplace.*

Antique Tin & Tole Ware ❧ 104 ❧

and the whalebone coming from the baleen whale was used in making spoons, boxes, stays for women's dresses, and household utensils. The ambergris was a valuable deposit that the whale gave out from the intestines, worth thousands of dollars for its use in perfumes. And the bones were used for various things, carved out by the men as they made the long journeys homeward after months of being away on their hazardous whaling trips. Pie crimpers are commonly found made of bone, and the busk for the front stay in a woman's dress was made of bone, delicately carved with hearts, initials, dates, and scrolls of various patterns. When carving was done on whalebone or on ivory, it was called "scrimshaw" and many are the collectors who gather such beautiful handwork of those early days.

Besides the sconces that hung in churches, there were many types of chandeliers, called candlebeams. These had a central arm and several branches, each holding a candle. They were made of tin, iron, or wood and some of them were elaborate in their designs. Few such chandeliers are to be seen today.

PLATE 200. *Also used on a whaling vessel was this inkwell. The drawer in its base held a candle and could be used as a candleholder. From the collection of Mrs. Herbert Hall of Worcester, Massachusetts.*

PLATE 201. *The side of this rare matchbox dropped open to become a candleholder. The grating in the bottom of the box was used to strike friction matches. From the collection of James A. Keillor.*

There is a rare candleholder, or chandelier, in my museum. This once hung in the cabin of the captain on a whaling vessel. It has a cylindrical center tube a foot long, tapering toward the top, four inches at the base and three at the top. It is fifteen inches long and is filled with sand to give it stability against the motions of the ship. From the center, four curved arms extend, each having a holder for a candle with a small removable plate or cup under it. Above the candles are four convex reflectors, attached on three-inch, horizontal arms that extend from the center tube. It hung by a ring on the top, slightly worn from long use.

From a whaling vessel came a rare tin inkwell. It measures about four inches long and two inches wide and holds a pen, ink, candle, sealing wax, and stamp. The box part has two inkwells, one now missing, and a groove that held the stamp for the sealing wax. Pulling out one side of the box brings out a second section. In this are two compartments, one with a hinged cover. At the end of the open compartment is a tin candleholder which held a candle used

PLATE 202. *Some large chandeliers held glass cups filled with oil. Half-inch candles were set in tiny wooden disks like those shown here and were floated in the glass cups. The circular holder with three cork floats was also used for the same purpose.*

a candle. A date on the inside of the cover reads 1835, along with an indistinct name. This must have been used on board ship, an airtight box to keep the matches dry.

Many were the varieties of candlestands, bringing the candle nearer to the person who was reading or sewing. The earliest holder was made as a wooden trammel which could be raised or lowered as the need arose, hanging near the manteltree or lintel. There was a tall wooden stand, sometimes with one arm for a candle and sometimes with two arms for two candles. Some of these have a threaded standard, others having holes into which a wooden pin was thrust to hold the arm. Early iron standards are found, too, made with tripod feet and one or two arms. Often there were holders for rushlights on these standards.

In the Stone House, the home of the Historical Society of Belchertown, Massachusetts, is an early tin holder for three candles. It has a conical base about six inches high, filled with sand to give it weight. The wire

to melt the sealing wax. A candle and a pen in the shape of a hand were found in the covered compartment. The stick of sealing wax is missing. After the letter had been written and sealed with sealing wax, the candle was extinguished and the drawer put back into place. A tiny lock shows that the box could be locked. The box is painted green and is in a collection of inkwells.

An unusual piece is the tin matchbox that was photographed for me. When opened, one side let down and there is a holder for

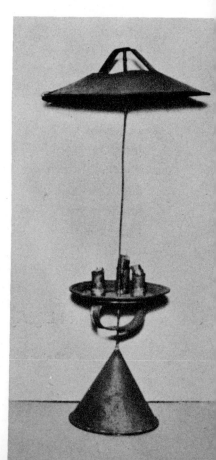

PLATE 203. *This candlestand has a base weighted with sand. The height of both the candleholder and the shade could be adjusted. From the Worcester Historical Society, Worcester, Massachusetts.*

PLATE 204. *Simple candlestands like this were suspended from the beams in old country stores. The conical base is filled with sand. From the Stone House, Belchertown, Massachusetts.*

standard is two feet long. Three candles are set into sockets on a plate that could be adjusted. Near the top is a shade to keep the heat of the flame from rising. This once hung from the ceiling in Longley's General Store in Belchertown in the late 1700's. Many rare pieces are found in such museums, preserved by their owners and given to a society where they may be seen by the many who come and go.

In my museum is a box of great value and of great interest to a collector. It was purchased at an auction on a rainy day and no one seemed to want it. Not having the slightest idea about the contents, I laid the box alongside the other boxes in my museum and waited for the day to come when I could learn more about what I had. It is an oval box about four inches long, made of thin wood glued together at the laps. There is a faint trace of what might have been a label at one time. The box holds tiny wooden discs into which are set tiny candles half an inch long. A pair of tin tweezers, coils of wax tapers, and a triangular tin holder with a thin piece of cork at the end of three tips make up the rest of the box. The holder with the three corks was placed in oil in glass cups that were part of the early church chandeliers. A wooden disc was placed on the triangular float with tweezers or the discs could have been set into the oil with no support under them. As the tiny candle burned, it drew the oil and continued to burn. The coils of wax tapers were extra, and the many discs in the box could have been fitted with more candles. This box and its contents seem to be rare, and the value has risen greatly from the thirty-five cents it cost me at the auction.

PLATES 205 & 206. *A rare "Bible lamp" was designed with a lid that could be closed, allowing the light from the candle to be cast only in a narrow field in front of the lamp. It is said to have been used when the reading of the Bible was proscribed.*

Mrs. Gillian Bailey of Harriman, New York, loaned me a few pieces from her museum for me to photograph. One was an unusual "Bible lamp," which came from England. There was a period in the history of England when the reading of the Bible was proscribed. In order to read it unseen after dark, this special lamp was constructed, holding a candle. After lighting the candle the hinged three-sided cover could be dropped over the open side, allowing the light to be cast only in a narrow field directly in front and below the lamp. Thus it minimized the risk of detection while providing sufficient light for reading.

An interesting device was a tarpot holder that kept the tar heated with a candle. This

PLATES 207 & 208. *This nurse's lamp is said to have been used during the Civil War. The perforated base holds a two-burner oil lamp. The kettle and cup fit together into the top of the lamp.*

stands a foot high and holds a pot of tar and a stick to apply the tar, used when treating fruit trees.

A nurse's lamp is occasionally found complete. Such a lamp was used to heat tea, coffee, or milk. The museum boasts of two such lamps, one said to have been used in the days of the Civil War. The body has fine perforations to allow the air to circulate for the flame of the two-burner oil lamp. The lamp sets in a circular holder that can be raised or lowered by a screw set on the outside. On the lamp are two tin caps, fastened with a chain, used to snuff out the flame. In the opening at the top of the lamp is a tin dish with a short handle, that held water. Fitting into that is a small

PLATES 209 & 210. *Two views of a tarpot holder used to keep the tar heated. The long cylindrical lamp that was placed in the base of the holder held a candle. From the collection of Mrs. G.W.B. Bailey.*

teakettle, slightly over four inches in diameter. This lamp and a tin warming pan started my collection of tinware, added to that of woodenware and ironware.

A different type of milk warmer or nurse's lamp has two extending ears for air vents. Stencilling is on the body and the handle. In this lamp there is a pan for hot water and another one for the milk or other drinks. The heat was made by a candle in a holder resting in the bottom. The candleholder could be taken out of the lamp, and the tip end stuck into the space between the lamp and the pan. The candle thus lighted the way about the house, serving two purposes, providing both heat and light. Another such lamp has a door on hinges into which an oil lamp was placed. This has a design of a flower, stencilled on the lamp and on the door. And in the Gwinn collection is a very artistic lamp with ear vents and two graceful side handles. This seems to

PLATES 213 & 214. *Two early nurse's lamps from the Gwinn collection of Philadelphia, and from the collection of Mrs. Frederick Nelson. The latter is built like the milk warmer and used an oil burner.*

be earlier than the stencilled lamps and of the same period as the one with the teakettle.

A later lamp is the one used when travelling. Inside the large tin cup is a two-burner oil lamp, with two snuffer caps on a chain. When the lamp was used, it was taken out of the cup holder and the cup

PLATES 211 & 212. *Two views of a decorated milk warmer. The larger holder on the right held water, which was heated by a candle placed in the conical holder with the handle. The candle was also used for light.*

PLATES 215 & 216. *An ingenious lamp is this travelling lamp. The two-burner oil lamp fits inside the cup with a lid. The handles of the cup are designed so that they fold flat around the contour of the cup.*

was placed on the frame of the lamp. The cup has two long wire handles that folded flat when packed. Other creations are probably found in diverse places, all made in the period preceding and following the Civil War.

In the Gay Nineties, a common event was the torchlight procession. This always happened at the time of some particular political celebration. Each man had a torch, a tin lamp burning kerosene, swinging in a bracket on the end of a pole, carried over his shoulder. It was quite a sight to see masses of men in costume marching in file through the city's main street.

Friction for making a spark has been obtained down the years among the various races in many ways. Among the primitives, friction was made between two sticks, one twirled upon the other, to make a spark in tinder placed around the point of contact. The bow drill was another means of producing a spark, one such drill is pictured. A stick was used with the cord of the bow twisted around it once. This stick rested on tinder, and when the bow was drawn back and forth, it twirled the stick which was held against another board with tinder around it. The heat resulting from the friction was enough to light the tinder. There is a ratchet turn by the handle to tighten the cord after it had been wound around the stick.

A commonly known gadget in the early homes was the tinderbox. This is a round, covered tin box with a handle and a holder on the cover for a candle. Inside the box is a thin cover with a ring handle, a piece of flint, and a metal striker. In the bottom

PLATE 218. *Bow drills like this were developed to start a fire. The cord of the bow was wound once around the wooden drill, which was placed vertically against a board. By pulling the bow back and forth, the stick was made to rotate against the board.*

PLATE 217. *Wooden drills were used by the Indians to start a fire from the heat generated by the friction of the drill against a wooden board.*

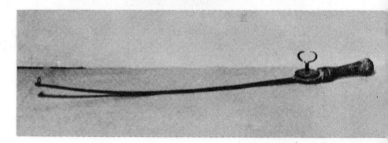

Antique Tin & Tole Ware ❧ 110 ❧

PLATE 219. *This unusual contraption is a cobbler's heating lamp, used for heating leather burnishers like the one shown here. From the Woodford Mansion of Philadelphia.*

PLATE 220. *After the invention of matches, match-safes were made for holding the matches. Shown here are three examples made of tin and one of wood.*

of the tinderbox in the museum are some charred bits of cotton. By striking the striker against the flint, a spark was produced while held over the tinder. The operation was not easily accomplished. With a flame in the tinder, the candle on the cover was lighted. The small cover snuffed out the flame in the tinder, the striker and flint were put back again and the box closed. Charles Dickens was quoted as saying, "if you had good luck, you could get a light in half an hour."

A tinder wheel was invented, spun like a top with a cord, making a spark in the tinder. Even powder was sometimes used, flashed in the pan of an old-fashioned gun with a flint lock. Matches such as are known in the present day came into common use in 1834. In England and France a friction match was produced in 1827, thin strips of wood coated with sulphur and tipped with a mixture of mucilage, chlorate of potash, and sulphide of antimony. This

match was called a lucifer for fairly obvious reasons. These were single matches and were not free from danger because of sparks. Brimstone matches were tipped with sulphur, made in square blocks or rows of

PLATE 221. *Tinderboxes were commonly used in the early homes before the invention of matches. Note the flint, U-shaped metal striker, and the tin lid used to smother the tinder once the candle had been lit from it.*

A Light after Dark

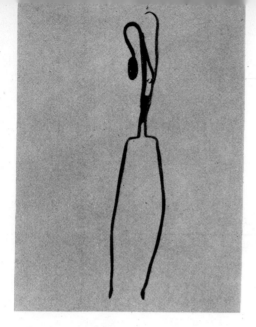

PLATE 222. *Pipe tongs like this were kept at hand near the fireplace for picking up live coals for lighting pipes. One arm of the tongs has a tamp to press down the tobacco, and the other has a hooked point to pick the bowl of the pipe.*

sheets. Both types are in the museum as they were purchased, wrapped in brown tissue paper. The wooden splints for matches were of pine or poplar.

Rather than resort to a striker and tinder, the men had pipe lighters, which were fashioned by the blacksmith. Some were called lazy tongs, having two scissor-like arms that extended to a distance of over a foot and folded back when closed. These reached out into the fire for a piece of live ember. Other pipe lighters did not extend. The tips were flattened out in order to pick up the embers. At the handle end was a tamp and a point, the tamp packed in the tobacco and the point picked it up if it had settled down too close. These were familiar, useful articles in the days of the open fireplaces.

CHAPTER FIVE

Our Heritage of Decorated Tinware

AMONG the various names of those early tinsmiths in New England, Zachariah Brackett Stevens stands for high achievement. He began sheet-tin works in Stevens Plains, now called Westbrook, Maine, in 1798, and he produced painted tinware, working until 1842, when commercial stores appeared.

It is claimed that Stevens at one time studied with Paul Revere, for it is known that he went to Boston to live for a few years. Paul Revere had a nephew, Phillip Rose, who later went to Stevens Plains to work as a tinsmith, which would further suggest some connection between the two men. Zachariah Stevens had two sons, Samuel and Alfred, who took over in 1830. Their work was not as carefully done as that of their father's. By 1832, there were eleven tinsmiths in the same locality and they sold as much as twenty-seven thousand dollars annually.

The type of tinware that was decorated included pincushion boxes, flower holders, cakeboxes, tea caddies or canisters, bread trays, and many other types of trays. The smaller trays were called tea trays and the larger ones, waiters, these having been the accustomed names in England. The pincushion box was an oblong box with a pincushion on the cover, sewed to the box through holes. This was a combination of sewing box and pincushion. Flower holders were like large cups on an inverted base or skirt. Moneyboxes were oblong, made in several sizes and often used for keeping trinkets. These were locked with a padlock, and valuable papers and documents were also kept in them. A group is shown here.

There were decorated bread trays, cracker trays, and apple trays, so named from the use to which the trays were put. The bread tray has straight sides and rolled ends, like that at the left of the illustration. The cracker tray is elliptical with pointed ends, and this was used for muffins as well as for crackers. Many an older person can recall that such a tray stood on the table in the dining room or in the kitchen, always kept filled with crackers so that anyone

PLATES 223 & 224. *Money or trinket boxes of tin were made in many sizes and shapes and were usually lavishly decorated. They were made with a hasp for a padlock.*

who was hungry might help himself. The apple tray is square and has four rolled sides and this, too, stood on the table filled with apples, from late summer on into the winter.

The decorations on these trays are of high order and seldom can duplicates be found. The designs were put on with stencils and by freehand. One tray illustrated is rare, made in the style of Chinese architecture, with a rolled edge and sides, on a low standard. Such a tray, which originated in England, was called a cheese coaster. This held the whole cheese which was served at the table. Originally, a coaster had wheels so that it could be rolled from one person to another; hence the word coaster to designate such a tray on a standard. Some tinware originated in the Far East, so naturally the styles of that section were copied. The design on this particular tray on a standard was done with stencils and freehand. A dainty cracker tray is illustrated that has latticed sides and handle holes, restored with a red lining and black outside.

Tea caddies or canisters of tin were made round, square, or oblong with a cap cover. These came in for decoration but with simple designs. Teapots and coffeepots were found among the decorated tinware. As has already been pointed out, the difference between the pot for tea and that for coffee was in the spout; that on a teapot was made in one piece and that for coffee in two pieces with a joint. A plate warmer such as the small type illustrated was decorated only slightly, the body having been painted yellow with a spray of fine flowers done in black. Match holders and candleholders were also decorated. Painting all such pieces was done partly to preserve the tin from rusting, which destroyed the article, and partly for artistic results.

The serving trays were perhaps the most popular and the most numerous of the decorated tinware. They were made in various shapes and sizes, each shape having a name applied to it. One of the oldest was the Chippendale tray, called also a Gothic tray from the Gothic style of England, with

PLATES 225 & 226. *The shapes of the trays varied with the type of objects they were designed to hold. The oblong tray on the left is a bread tray, the two oval ones were for crackers, and the square one on the right is an apple tray.*

scalloped edge. This edge was also called a piecrust edge. These trays were made of papier-mâché as well as of tin, and the decorations on them were of the highest order, such works being called toleware. The decorations showed fountains, the bird of paradise, flowers, fruits, and scenes from the Orient, where the trays of papier-mâché were first produced. The Chippendale period extended from 1750 to 1800. The Queen Anne tray, another type, has a scalloped edge but with rounded points instead of the sharper points of the Chippendale.

The lace-edge trays are beautiful specimens of early trays. They were made in both round and oval shapes and in graded sets. The narrow edges were pierced with square-, diamond-, and wedge-shaped tools. A few rectangular trays were made, with pierced sides and plain corners. A rare lace-edge cake basket is illustrated that has a narrow hinged handle, which was pierced, with pierced sides and plain corners with a decoration. This illustration shows square-shaped piercing in the sides and wedge-shaped on the rolled-over rims.

The lace-edge tray has been accredited to

PLATE 228. *Teapots and coffeepots were among the favorite household utensils that were decorated in color. Shown here are, from left to right, a coffeepot, syrup jug, and teapot, all once heavily decorated.*

PLATE 229. *Cheese coasters with rolled ends are seldom found. Whole cheeses were served at the table in coasters of this type.*

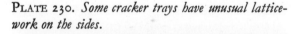

PLATE 227. *Canisters for tea and coffee were made in a variety of sizes and shapes. The square one in the middle is of a very early date.*

PLATE 230. *Some cracker trays have unusual lattice-work on the sides.*

⌊ 115 ⌋ *Our Heritage of Decorated Tinware*

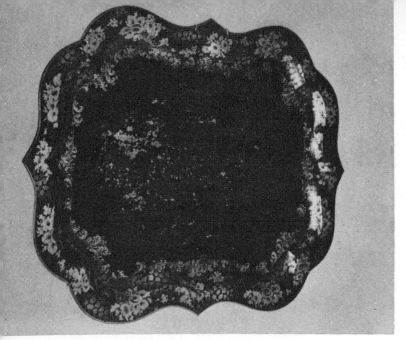

PLATE 231. *Serving trays were the most popular of the decorated tinware. Trays of this type with a piecrust edge are known as Chippendale trays. From the Andover Historical Society of Andover, Massachusetts.*

PLATE 232. *From the Concord Antiquarian Society comes this cake basket, an excellent example of the lace-edge work that was a popular means of decorating tinware.*

Paul Revere and is thus called a Paul Revere tray. Paul Revere was born in Boston in 1735 and began making lace-edge trays before the Revolutionary War, importing sheet tin from England. He trained apprentices in this work, and after the war he established a tin shop along with his other works in copper and silver.

Oval galley trays also were made by Paul Revere. Webster defines a galley tray as being "an oblong tray of wood or brass with upright sides, for holding type which has been set, or is to be made up." The tin galley trays are oval as well as oblong. They

have solid rails or rails with handle holes or pierced rails. The rails are narrow. Some galley trays have a very elaborate rail, with a combination of solid and pierced work. The piercing is often latticed or key-hole. The decorations on such trays follow those on any of the lace-edge trays. The typical galley trays are large trays, many being in the Concord Antiquarian Society, Concord, Massachusetts. They are as much as three feet long and are extremely heavy. Heavy trays are superior to those of light weight, showing the thickness of the sheet iron used in the tinning.

PLATE 233. *Many tin trays for the home were made like the galley trays used by the typesetter to carry pieces of type. This example, thirty inches in diameter, is from the Concord Antiquarian Society.*

PLATE 234. *These trays of French origin are often called "Paul Revere" trays. The tray on the right has an original flower and bud design.*

The octagonal trays were classed as country tinware, put out by rural tinsmiths, beginning about 1800. These have a narrow edge and were made in graded sizes, called more often coffin trays because of the fact that their shape resembled the ends of the early pine coffins. If such a tray has a seam in the middle, the reason is given that the tinsmith had no sheet large enough so he seamed two pieces together. It has been said that such seamed trays were sometimes made from two maple-syrup cans, peculiar to Vermont!

A kidney-shaped tray is not commonly found; the one shown here from my collection is painted red, with gold and black flowers. These have a narrow rolled edge. Oblong trays with rolled edges were made by 1840 in various sizes, first with no handle holes. Handle holes followed at a later date. Oval trays with narrow rolled edges and rounded corners appear to be the last type of tray to be made.

Snuffer trays were made to hold the snuffers which every family needed in the days of candles. These trays vary in shape and size; oblong, boat-shaped, coffin-shaped, and Chippendale, most of them a little longer than the snuffer itself. Silver snuffers rested on silver trays, but the ordinary snuffer of steel rested on a decorated tin tray. The designs were daintily executed.

Many elaborate pieces of tinware were brought from China, such as tea chests of various sizes, tin and papier-mâché trays with mother-of-pearl insets, and many receptacles, none of these as severely plain as the tinware of England and America.

The art of japanning was taken from China. This was was done in England starting about 1780 by craftsmen who

PLATE 235. *A kidney-shaped tray is rare. This is a beautiful example, painted red with black and gold decorations.*

imitated the Oriental lacquer work of the sixteenth, seventeenth, and eighteenth centuries. The tin article was covered with a coat of asphaltum and placed in a drying or annealing oven for hardening. Asphaltum varnish is a solution of mineral asphalt in varnish which produces a shiny, brownish-black effect, partially transparent. When diluted with varnish, various tones of golden brown are produced over the bright tin. Such work was done on trays, boxes, tea caddies, and other articles. In Boston, one Nehemiah Partridge was using this method of decorating as early as 1711.

In England, decorated tinware was made

PLATE 236. *These two trays are examples of what were known as "coffin trays" because of the resemblance of their octagonal shapes with that of the early coffins.*

PLATE 237. *Spice cases like this early example with elaborate decorations in color were used in old country stores. This case is six feet long and is now in the Wiggins Country Store of Northampton, Massachusetts.*

in Pontypool, Usk, Wolverhampton, Birmington, and Aldermanbury, and thousands of finished trays were exported yearly, especially from Pontypool. Many such trays were copied by tinsmiths in America. At one time when china factories in England were forced to shut down, the decorators went over to tinware manufacturers, using the same designs that had been used on china. That gave tinware a greater number of designs and gave a tremendous impetus to the industry.

In 1770, William and Edward Patterson, natives of Ireland, came to Berlin, Connecticut. Some records spell the name "Pattison," and Edward changes to "Edgar." And in fact there was a branch of the family that spelled its name "Pattison" who went further south, while the "Pattersons" remained in Connecticut. Those two brothers made large quantities of tinware and supplied tin peddlers with it. In the same town was a Hiram Mygatt, who had a shop in the rear of his premises for japanning tinware. This was in the year 1780 and on.

There were designs peculiar to Pennsylvania and to New England. Pennsylvania colors appear to be bolder, more like the colors of the peasant designs of Europe, with certain characteristic strokes. Pennsylvania used unicorns, birds, tulips, pomegranates, angels, horses, people, as well as geometric patterns. They decorated tinware and furniture, especially their chests. New England produced work more vivid than that of Pennsylvania, using mostly native fruits and flowers for designs. It would seem as if the migrating of the apprentices

PLATES 238 & 239. *Two views of a rare "Home Economizer." A special place was provided for all the common spices, condiments, and staples for the kitchen. It is two feet high, with colored designs, and is from the mid nineteenth century. From the collection of Edward Durell of Columbus, Ohio.*

PLATES 240 & 241. *Two examples of early decoration work on oblong trays. The design of fruit and flowers on the tray on the left is quite rare. It is done in full color, using blue, white, red, green, and gold. The border design is stencilled, combined with touches of freehand work.*

had much to do with local characteristics. Most of these artists came from Connecticut and they spread their work throughout New England.

Tinware was decorated with stencilling as well as with freehand painting. Stencilling dates back to the early days of civilization, as has been found in historical research work. And the methods that were used on toleware did not differ very much from the earlier examples. This was done by applying paint or bronze through cutouts, using a pouncer dipped in the paint. This pouncer was a wad of cotton batting or sheep's wool, covered with velvet or chamois.

The colors used were the old pumpkin yellow, yellow ochre, Indian red, gray, brown, a peculiar black, Prussian blue, and white. The work was done in both colored bronzes and oil paints. Designs included fruits, flowers, birds, animals, houses, trees, boats, and people, including children. Many of these designs were taken from foreign lands, showing either that the tinware came from foreign shores or that such foreign designs were copied.

Toleware is the name given to the work of the highest order. The designs are elaborate and finely executed; the fountain, the bird of paradise, country scenes depicting villages, houses, churches, castles, people, animals, and scenes from nature, done in delicate shades of gold and in superb coloring.

PLATE 242. *Sugar was molded and sold in tall conical shapes. The odd nippers were used for cutting the sugar cones. The tin container is a sugar bowl with decorations characteristic of its Pennsylvania origin.*

Our Heritage of Decorated Tinware

In my family is a large octagonal tray with handle holes which has a design of exotic flowers and fruits on the rim. This tray once carried food from a slaves' kitchen into the dining room of the family, in a seaport town in Connecticut, more than a hundred years ago. There is also a pair of small octagonal trays that were used to serve the master his wine before meals, in a town near Boston. These two small trays have the rare center finish called "tortoise shell," with shining

PLATE 243. *An early tray with an exotic design of flowers and fruit on the border. It is said to have carried food from the slaves' kitchen to the master's room in a seaport town of Connecticut.*

PLATE 245. *The two small trays on the top have the rare finish called "tortoise shell" in their centers. Shining patches of silver leaf show through the top coating of asphaltum covered with alizarin crimson.*

patches of silver leaf showing through the asphaltum, covered with a fiery coat of alizarin crimson.

Our decorated snuffer trays are used as pencil holders. Small lace-edge trays hold sugar and cream at a social gathering, while a large tray holds the coffee urn and cups. One beautiful oblong box has the original padlock, showing that it once held valuables that were carefully locked away. Uncle George's Liverpool travelling tin with the blue lining holds some of my most important correspondence. A decorated coffee-pot sits atop our old secretary along with the large tray that came from Connecticut. The family cakebox has lost all trace of its decoration because it served for many years, opened and shut by us children as

PLATE 244. *This large Chippendale tray is a beautiful example of the elaborately decorated toleware. The exquisite design of flowers and bird of paradise are done in full color, with touches of gold. From the collection of Mrs. Mary Johnson.*

Antique Tin & Tole Ware ❧ 120 ❧

we took pieces of cake, either forbidden or allowed. All this is unwritten history of our family tinware.

Gathering tinware and learning how to decorate it has become one of the most popular phases in collecting antiques. Experienced teachers are training eager students in every quarter and it not only means a happy pastime but it gives the owner many pieces of tinware for his own enjoyment. Reproductions in all types of tinware are flooding the market, and the antique collector does well to know the difference between the old and the new. The workmanship in making the tray is different.

In the first place, the new trays are made of heavy sheet iron, tinned, regardless of what size or shape they are. They are painted black, the better to sell. The edge is rolled over a wire like in the old trays, but it also is too perfect a job to appear handmade. The edge of the old tray does not roll but

PLATE 246. *This is the old cakebox that has been in use for years in the family. Most of the decoration and design has come off after much use.*

has a narrow flat hem after it is turned over the wire.

When handle holes were made in an oblong tray, the workmanship of the new and old are noticeably different. The narrow edge of the hole of the new is turned up onto the upper side of the tray. In the old trays, the edge is turned back onto the bottom side of the tray. The cutting in the new tray is perfect as if done by a marking tool. In the old, it is done by hand and

PLATE 247. *From Pontypool in England came some of the most beautiful examples of toleware. These pieces are all Pontypool toleware now in the Cooper Union of New York.*

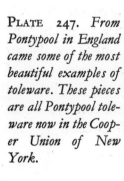

PLATES 248 & 249. *This unusual biscuit box was made toward the end of the nineteenth century for the biscuit manufacturers of Huntley & Palmers, Ltd. Courtesy of the Tin Research Institute of Middlesex, England.*

often the hole is not cut straight with the side of the tray. The new lace-edge trays have a different pattern than that of the old. Those of the new are varied and fancy. Those of the old are either pie- or wedge-shaped, diamond-shaped, or square. The edges of the new lace-edge trays turn up abruptly; those of the old have slanting sides, sometimes with a slight roll.

The corners of the new oblong trays are cut close and welded together. In the old trays, the seams are made by lapping over the part that was left when cutting out the pattern, making an extra piece which is welded. In the new apple trays and cracker trays, not only are the side seams cut close and welded, but the bottom is welded on as an extra piece. In the old trays, the tin is shaped as one piece, bottom and sides, the seams lapped over and welded. Some of the new small trays in the Chippendale

or oblong shapes have no rolled edge. It would not have been possible to make an edge roll over a wire if the piece of tin were small. Many designs are made in the new trays and other articles, all new creations and never found in the old trays.

It is interesting to note here that when I first became enthusiastic about antique shops in 1933, I had a friend who bought and decorated any and all tinware. She was the daughter of my adopted grandmother. I took her in my car to many shops in many states, and as she discussed tinware with the owners, I listened. I absorbed much unconsciously. This perhaps accounts for my interest in decorated tinware today and my knowledge, even though limited, of the art of decorating. My friend accuses me of having said in those first years, "I have no use for antiques." It would seem as if flat statements were better left unsaid!

CHAPTER SIX

The Tin Peddler & His World

MUCH LORE surrounds the peddlers of the horse-and-buggy days of the Gay Nineties. Even though those days might not be within our memory, the many stories about them can never be forgotten, stories that tell of the colorful life of those men who took to the road peddling sundry wares.

While peddling was on its way out, in the Gay Nineties, there were many peddlers who went afoot or with a cart with their goods, serving the families at the back door. Stores, the source of supplies, were numerous, but often it would be a long trudge to go to purchase the family's needs, so peddlers were many times a blessing. Tramps were distinguished from peddlers, for a tramp asked for something to eat, perhaps returning the favor by doing odd jobs about the place. Peddlers might sometimes look like tramps, but they had something to sell and, more often than not, it was something that was needed.

How dear to my heart are the memories of the peddlers who regularly appeared at our back door back in those days: Aunt Betsy, the ancient colored woman, with her homemade bluing, who rested on the top step of our piazza, "Jes to res' ma weary bone.' I's more'n a hundre' years ole"; the deaf, one-armed sewing-silk man with his boxes of colored spools in infinite variety; the horseradish man, who dipped his condiment out of a wooden bucket with a tin scoop; the hulled-corn man with his delicious steamed yellow corn in a pail.

Many a peddler's cart passed our front gate in the city or upcountry in those leisurely days: the small, white covered wagons of the fish and meat peddlers drawn by one horse; the little cart of the cracker man who always gave me an enormous acorn-shaped cooky; the two-wheeled push wagon of the busy scissors grinder. Here also passed the long wagon with the tall side racks piled high with stepladders and piazza furniture in the natural wood. We often saw a load of barrels stacked in the wagon built like a hay wagon that had staves extending upward from the sides.

Remember the old saying "To see a load of barrels is a sign of rain"?

In those days, the popcorn man used to push a two-wheeled cart ahead of him and whenever there was a band concert in some park, the popcorn man was sure to be there. The cart had a big glass enclosure and inside was a gas burner on which a wire corn popper rested while the corn was popped. The fire was provided by a tube of compressed gas. A tin pitcher of melted butter and a big, tin salt shaker was part of the equipment of the cart, and after the corn was scooped into a small bag with a tin scoop, butter and salt were used freely. Popcorn was quite a treat, and five cents a bag seemed a lot to spend in those days.

Another familiar peddler was the hokey-pokey ice-cream man who used to go through the streets, ringing his bell and selling his stuff. His trade was never rushing and, with only five-cent sales, the man never could have had a big income. We had an ice-cream freezer of heavy tin. On every holiday, Sunday, and birthday, we had either ice cream or lemon sherbet. One of the menfolk put the ice into a burlap bag and pounded it with the head of an axe. Then the cooked custard was poured into the inner can, and that was placed in the wooden freezer, standing outside by the

PLATE 250. *The fish peddler could easily be recognized by the sounds of his tin horn.*

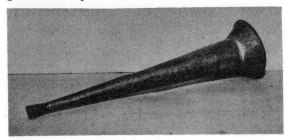

PLATE 251. *The scissors grinder was among the many peddlers who travelled from town to town. This is a woodcut by Alexander Anderson that appeared in the* Cries of New York, *New York, 1808.*

cellar door. The chopped ice was packed all around the can, mixed with freezing salt, the top part with the crank clamped on, and slowly the churning was begun. The frozen mixture had to be tested a few times to be sure the ice cream or sherbet was doing well, and, when it was done, the dasher was pulled out of the tin can, the cover placed back on again, and a burlap bag thrown over the whole thing to remain until dinnertime. We children always begged to have some ice cream left on the dasher so we could have a big taste before dinner.

Before the blight struck down the chestnut trees, a common sight was a vender standing on a street corner selling roasted chestnuts. He had an arrangement that was like a brazier of the old days, with a charcoal fire inside. Many families roasted chestnuts in a wire popper over a fire in the fireplace or over the coals in a stove. We did that!

Numerous as these peddlers were in the Gay Nineties, they were gradually supplanted by stores. That colorful era faded into history, and the next generation knew those peddlers only by the tales that were told.

In the early days previous to the Gay

Nineties nearly every family could supply its own household necessities. The various members could make the shoes, weave the cloth, make the garments, butcher the animals, and do many of the other duties necessary to keep a family together. But quite probably some of the families were not skilled in all of these lines, and it was then that the itinerant workers took over some of the jobs. They were always welcome, for they were good company and brought much news in those days of little communication. One of the most important of these itinerant workers was the shoemaker who came in the winter to make shoes and to repair them. He went from house to house, carrying his workbench on his back or in a cart and he often remained an entire week with each family while he made the shoes. He had his meals and his lodging. The family provided the leather either from tanned hides of their own animals or from the local tannery where the farm animals had been bartered. Often more shoes were made than were required by the family and these the cobbler took away with him to sell or barter to another family. All the shoes were hand-sewn until 1811, when wooden shoe pegs were used, whittled from birch saplings.

Since making shoes was only winter work, the shoemaker farmed in the spring and summer. The shoemaker was good company; he could sing, play the fiddle, or tell stories and thus helped out in the town's social life in the winter evenings. The family eagerly looked forward to his coming. The shoemaker not only brought gossip but he added to it as he moved along from one family to another throughout the village.

There is a little old house up in New Hampshire that has a small additional room at one end that used to be a cobbler's shop. Someone in the family took up the trade of cobbling and the village folk brought their work to him. Such shops followed the days of itinerant cobblers. As the years went on, the making of shoes became an industry, and the trade of those itinerant workers expanded into manufacturing establishments.

The house that my Uncle George bought, near Worcester, started out as a cobbler's shop early in 1800. The original owner built an eight-room house for himself and his family, making his workshop in one of the rooms after the shoeshop in the yard had burned down. No cellar is under the original one-room shop, the part that was built before the additional rooms for the house. When my uncle bought the house, he made more changes, changing the outside paint from pumpkin yellow to coffin red. Coffin red is the name of an early red paint that was made from red clay. It was commonly used to paint coffins, as it was a good preservative. Only the town records state that the bootshop was once in the west corner of that yellow house, the part that has no cellar under it.

The women often had help with their weaving. Every family grew flax and raised sheep and owned a loom for weaving linen and woolen materials. Because of the many demands upon the womenfolk, an itinerant weaver was often called upon to help out.

A field of flax and of hemp was planted in the spring and by late June or July was ready to be picked and prepared for the winter weaving. The process of preparing this flax and hemp was long and difficult and required many weeks. The final step was to spin the threads on a flax wheel.*

The sheep were sheared in the early spring, often with the help of itinerant shearers, and the wool went through a long process of preparing it for the spinning wheel, where it was made into woolen threads for weaving. Then the flax and the wool were made into skeins, some of which were put into the dye tub and colored, wound on bobbins and quills for the shuttles, ready for the itinerant weaver. He wove materials for garments and household articles and often wove the coverlets for beds, so popular at that time.

Following the weaver came the maker of garments, supplying the entire family with clothing. The tailor was sometimes called a gooseherder, for he carried a heavy, long, and narrow iron for pressing, that was known as a goose. In families of wealth, living in the South or on the seacoast, the manteau-maker came to make gowns, hats, and cloaks for the women.

In the fall of the year, the animals were slaughtered. Sometimes the animals were driven off to a slaughterhouse, but more often they were slaughtered on the farm, with the help of an itinerant butcher. The meat was stored in barrels of brine. Very little fresh meat was eaten. Slabs of ham were smoked in smoke ovens and packed in bins with charcoal or oats, to preserve them through the winter months.

Then it was that there was much fat on hand to be made into tallow for candles. Often the itinerant butcher was also the candlemaker, combining the two trades. In

* Gould, *The Early American House.*

exchange for butchering and making candles, he took fat in addition to the meals and lodging he received while he worked at each house. With this fat he made candles, and these he sold as he went on his way to other towns. The candlemaker had his own molds. The story of candlemaking has been told in a previous chapter and it shows how dependent the families were upon candles for light in the homes until kerosene appeared.

The cooper went his rounds making and repairing woodenware. Boxes, buckets, churns, barrels, and woodenware for the table such as plates and bowls were made by the itinerant cooper if the man of the house was not handy with his tools. The cooper returned each season to restock the family and to repair whatever woodenware needed mending. A cooper-shop often began its life out in a back yard. Here the cooper made his wares and repaired and mended, and here the village people came to buy or to bring their broken utensils, including tankards, kegs, and funnels.*

Pewterware was used in the home extensively from 1750 until well into the nineteenth century. This had to be mended or replaced, and it was the tinker who performed that work. At the time of the Revolutionary War much of the pewter was taken and made into bullets, which accounts for the loss of many of the early pewter receptacles.

Doctors, dentists, photographers, and portrait painters were on the road for many years, making a living by carrying on their trade in the homes. They remained many days, working for the entire family.

* Gould, *Early American Wooden Ware.*

Peddlers were an important group in the pattern of life in the eighteenth and nineteenth centuries. They were called chapmen and first went on foot carrying two tin trunks, filled with goods, slung over their shoulders by means of a webbing harness or a leather strap. It is little wonder that most of the peddlers came from New England, because the climate of that section made the people quick-witted, industrious, and adventurous. In contrast were the people of the South, who were easygoing. Thus we find it was the New England peddler who began selling on the road, and many of these young men later became founders of stores of national repute.

Because the homes could not supply the necessary commodities, it was but natural that these young peddlers thought out a way of taking the goods to the families. Among the noted men who began life as a peddler was Bronson Alcott, born in 1799 and living a span of eighty-nine years. His parents had chosen a career for him, expecting him to go to college, but Bronson announced that he was going to be a peddler. It was a common thing to make a big profit and this attracted energetic young men. As much as two hundred per cent profit was sometimes realized. Bronson, whose full name was Amos Bronson Alcott, was born in Wolcott, Connecticut. On his first venture as a peddler he went to New Jersey and worked farther south, selling almanacs and later tinware from a tin trunk. Returning from his first year with a big profit, he was joined by his brother Chatfield, who went with him on his second journey. This was not successful, nor was the third trip, which was made with a cousin William.

Many instances of young men who made good in life are recorded in history. One particular New England young man was John Boynton, who began as a peddler and later in life, with much money and a desire to help youth, founded the Worcester Polytechnical Institute in Worcester, Massachusetts. Jonas G. Clark, born in Hubbardston, Massachusetts, set up a store in Lowell and a second one in Milford, both in his native state, and sold tinware. Later, he acquired real estate in California and in New York and when he later sold his land in lots he became a wealthy man. His name is perpetuated by a university where both young men and young women benefit from this endowed institution, Clark University. There is a peddler's cart in an outlying town that Clark once used, when he sold his tinware from his store.

My minister-uncle Ed—I had two uncles who were ministers—used to say as a boy that he would be a tin peddler some and a minister some. The tin peddler's cart seemed to fascinate all young boys. But the minister part won out, for Uncle Ed never seemed to have any knack for selling or bartering.

Alice Morse Earle records a story of Chepa Rose, a trunk peddler who went through New England for forty-eight years, appearing at every farmhouse throughout Narragansett and eastern Connecticut, "at intervals as regular as the action and appearance of the sun, moon and tides; and everywhere he was greeted with an eager welcome." Again she says, "He was a famous medicine brewer; from the roots and herbs and barks that he had gathered as he tramped along the country roads he manufactured a cough medicine that was twice as effective and twice as bitter as old Dr. Greene's; he made famous plasters of two kinds, plaster to stick and plaster to crawl, the latter to follow the course of the disease or pain; he concocted wonderful ink; he showed Jenny Greene how to bleach her new straw bonnet with sulphur fumes; he mended umbrellas, harnesses, and tinware; he made glorious teetotums which the children looked for as eagerly and unfailingly as they did for his tops and marbles, his ribbons and his Gibraltars." Thus we learn of a typical peddler of the early nineteenth century.

The tin trunks were filled with what were known as Yankee notions, such as pins, needles, hooks and eyes, scissors, razors, combs, coat and vest buttons, spoons, cotton goods, laces, and perfumes.* Tin peddlers were taxed as early as 1700.

There were also peddlers of clocks. Often these clocks he peddled were merely the works of a clock without a case that hung on the wall and were called a "wag on the wall." Many stories are told about the various means the peddler had in putting across a sale. One story is of a man who sold ten clocks on his trip and had one left. He promised each customer that if the clock would not go properly, he would give them another. So with one clock left, he began his tour again, backward. He found the last clock he had sold was not going properly, so he exchanged it for the clock he had left, saying it was all he had on hand. Taking number ten clock, he called on customer number nine, saying he had one clock left and he would leave that. At number eight clock, he left number nine

* Richardson Wright, *Hawkers and Walkers in Early America.*

clock and thus he continued until every customer had a different clock. The story, however, does not continue and tell how the exchanged clocks behaved nor how the peddler fared in the end!

Eli Terry, the famous clockmaker, began making clocks in 1793 at Plymouth, Connecticut, near Waterbury. The various parts were cut out of hard wood and finished with a file. The hemp cords were spun by women who used their own flax. Twice a year, Terry peddled his clocks, going as far as the Hudson, carrying four at a time, one in front of the saddle, one on either side and one at the back. These were packed in a travelling bag such as was used on horseback, called a portmanteau. Terry sold his first clocks for from twenty to forty dollars. By 1807, a company was formed, and five hundred clocks were manufactured at one time, using water power and steam. Then the clocks went out in covered wagons, drawn by two horses, travelling south for quick trade. Seth Thomas, another man whose name is synonymous with famous clocks, became a partner to Terry. By 1837, brass began to be used and wood was discontinued. By 1840, 100,000 clocks were made in one year and peddled.

Simon Willard, still another man who became famous in the clock world, made banjo clocks, both a large size and a junior size. These were so named because their shape resembled a banjo. Willard peddled his clocks himself until a factory took over and the sales were made by a group of peddlers. These clock peddlers not only made clocks but repaired clocks that they found on their routes. All clock peddlers became proficient in repairing.

PLATE 252. *This scale model of a tin peddler's cart with its carload of sundry household goods is in the Society for the Preservation of New England Antiquities. Note the steelyard hanging from the rear extension of the cart.*

Because of the poor conditions that allowed little travelling, it was but natural that the early peddlers went on foot. Then when better roads were a general thing, the peddler rode on a horse. Eventually it was a cart or a wagon that drew the peddler's things, and thus came the peddlers who could carry wares of much size.

A peddler was called a pack peddler when he carried his pack of wares on his back. These peddlers often frightened little children because of the grotesque-looking pack and their shabby appearances. When riding on a horse, a peddler could carry spinning wheels and set them up upon arrival at a home. He could carry woodenware for the kitchen and brooms, chairs, and farm implements, such as winnowing sieves, corn shellers, splint cheese-baskets. He carried spices and dyes, which were greatly needed in the home, for spices were used in preserving and pickling, and dyes were used when coloring woolen skeins for weaving garments and household goods.

Tinware had begun to be made by 1780 and was carried first on foot in tin trunks and later on horseback. By the beginning of the nineteenth century the wares to be sold increased rapidly, a wagon came to be used and then the era of the "tin peddler and his cart" began to dawn. Quite commonly, the spelling is "pedlar." Bronson Alcott wrote in his diary at the end of each day and recorded his daily activities as a "pedlar," spelt as it was in England.

The tin peddler's cart was a light truck with four wheels, drawn by one horse or sometimes by two horses. As a rule it was painted red. The body was built like a box with a seat at the front with a high dashboard. At the side of the boxed body were compartments, small square ones toward the front and long ones toward the back, with doors that lifted, fastened with a hasp that could be padlocked. In these compartments were carried small trinkets and merchandise that needed protection from the elements. At the back end was an extension,

PLATES 253 & 254. *In the Farmer's Museum of Hadley, Massachusetts is this old peddler's cart. It was made for two horses. Note the many built-in compartments, boxes, and shelves for carrying the merchandise.*

two or three feet wide, like a platform on which could be stacked various bulky things. From the back extended an arm that held the steelyard or scales and also a sharp-pointed rod fastened in an upright position onto which sheep pelts were thrust. A rack for brooms was on one side.

In the Farmer's Museum in Hadley, Massachusetts, is housed a fine peddler's cart. Made for a pair of horses, it was painted red with yellow underparts, and has wooden

PLATE 255. *An etching titled "The Tin Peddler's Call" appeared in the* Harper's Weekly *of June 20th, 1868.*

axles and wooden springs. The driver's seat has a long compartment at either end, with doors that lift. The dasher is curved and the floor lifts up and provides more storage room. Under the box compartment by the side of the driver is another square compartment. The body of the cart is like a long box with two long doors on either side, that lift. Inside is a space that runs through from side to side, and a long tray slides on rods. This tray could have been reached from either side of the cart. It is only half as wide as the cart and when pushed over the peddler could reach down into the deep compartment below. Articles could be stored on top of the cart, which is fenced in with a narrow rail. At the back is a rack that could be dropped or closed, held by leather straps on which could be carried heavy things. This cart came from Brattleboro, Vermont, but little is known about it.

The tin peddler's stock consisted of pins, needles, scissors, combs, buttons, and sewing thread. There were also cotton stuffs, dry goods, children's books, straw hats, shoes, brooms, all kinds of tinware, woodenware, jackknives, razors, tow cloth for Southern slaves, knitted goods, snuffboxes, tobacco, brushes, and spectacles with tin or copper

Antique Tin & Tole Ware ❧ 130 ❧

frames. The tin peddler in the early days took no money, but made his sales by bartering. Thus he received things at his own price, things on which no value could be placed, such as furniture, glass, china, and pewter, much to his advantage. On the return trip, the cart would be loaded with linen rags, wool, skins with the wool on and those with the wool off, hog bristles for brushes, pelts of various sorts, old and worn-out household utensils of copper, brass, and pewter, and other household articles.

Important barter items were the linen rags and the wood ashes; the source of two important industries. The manufacture of fine writing paper from linen rags was started by the house of Crane and Company of Dalton, Massachusetts. The rags for this new industry were furnished by the peddlers. Wood ashes went into the making of lye, which was an important ingredient of soap. Thus it was the peddler who was the go-between of the housewife's supply of rags and ashes and the products made from them.

The story of Ivory soap reads like a fairy story. Two men, William Proctor and James Gamble founded the company in the fall of 1837. William Proctor at the age of thirty-six began a candle factory, and James Gamble began a small soap business. The two men married sisters, and the father-in-law suggested a partnership, making both soap and candles. They made the soap in two large cauldrons and used fat from homes, hotels, and packing houses. Wood ashes were obtained from peddlers, and lye for the soap was made by leaching the ashes. Twelve frames of soap were made each week, each frame weighing a thousand pounds. The two men peddled their soap through the streets in a wheelbarrow. The story of the rapid development of the business and the final naming of the soap is attractively told in a booklet put out by Proctor and Gamble.*

The brass industry was started when the peddler collected old copper and brass utensils, which had once been brought from the countries across the water. These were turned into sheet brass from which came brass buttons, lamps, kettles, cowbells, and various buckles for harnesses, breeches, and shoes.

Tin peddlers and tinsmiths worked in close cooperation with each other. It was the tinsmith who kept the supply of tinware ahead of the demands for it. There were two main sources of this output in New England, one in Stevens Plains, Maine, near Portland and the other in Berlin, Connecticut.

We have already noted the activities of Zachariah Stevens, the early Maine tinsmith, who worked on tinware until his death in 1856. It is claimed that he had studied with Paul Revere. His specialty was oblong boxes of various sizes, fruit containers, cakeboxes, and flowerpots. His two sons, Samuel and Alfred, followed him but did not execute the same fine work. By 1832, there were eleven tin shops in the same locality near Portland. This ware went out in tin carts.

It is said that between 1800 and 1835 there were more young men born and brought up in Maine who graduated from the "tin carts" than graduated from Bowdoin College in the same time. And there were less failures

* Proctor and Gamble, *Into a Second Century*.

in life among these peddlers than there were among the college graduates.

In Berlin, Connecticut, there were two brothers, William and Edward Patterson. They imported sheet tin from England and made it into cooking utensils. These they sold from door to door in Berlin. They even walked to nearby settlements, trudging with their tin trunks loaded with tin utensils. Tin was shiny and attractive and soon replaced pewter, which gave a very drab effect in those early homes. It was a continuous task to keep pewter polished, but tin needed only to be washed, and tin utensils could easily be replaced by new ones.

The factories in Connecticut were located along streams, which furnished water power. Berlin became the center of the tin industry, which continued until 1850. It is estimated that ten thousand boxes of sheet tin were imported from England each year. The ware was taken on foot, on horseback, and then in the cart.

The tin peddler covered as much as twelve to fifteen hundred miles on a single trip, going to the South, the West, and to Canada. Their trip began in late summer or in the winter. The tin workers in Berlin would pile up large stocks through the spring and summer months, which the peddlers loaded onto their carts. Then these tinsmiths would be sent to various towns in the South, taking their tools and templets with them, where they would make up another supply. They remained all winter putting out their tinware. The peddlers planned their routes so when they finished their stock of supplies, they were in the vicinity of one of these towns: Richmond, Charleston, and Savannah in the South; Albany in New York; as well as in a number of towns in eastern Canada to the north. The peddlers handed over their profits to an agent and restocked from the new utensils. Then they started for the spring and summer trips. Selling out once more, they returned to Connecticut by fall.

On the northern routes, the peddlers started in the early spring, and the tinsmiths went to their temporary factories some time during the summer months. Filling up the carts again, the peddlers headed toward home, selling their stock as they travelled. They all headed for New York. There they sold their empty carts and their horses, had a gay celebration, and went back to Connecticut by boat. A carefree, vagabond life for the young, adventurous men whose training was in the school of life.

By 1860, railroads, highways, and river traffic largely supplanted the tin cart as a means for transporting the stock of the factories and carrying it into the markets. The peddler continued to take a store in miniature to his customers, often including remnants and factory seconds, but when large stores appeared in the various cities throughout the country, the peddler and his cart were doomed. Museums show the cart that once travelled with its merchandise, and historians tell of the life of those peddlers, but their doom came with the advent of the mechanical age and the high-pressure salesmanship of the twentieth century.

Index

NOTE: *Italic* numbers refer to pages on which relevant plates appear.